Straight Parents
Gay Children

◆

Straight Parents
Gay Children

———————— ◆ ————————

Keeping Families Together

Robert A. Bernstein

THUNDER'S MOUTH PRESS

First edition
First printing, 1995

Published by
Thunder's Mouth Press
632 Broadway, 7th Floor
New York, NY 10012

LIBRARY OF CONGRESS CATALOGING-IN-PUBLICATION DATA
Bernstein, Robert, 1926-
    Straight parents/gay children : keeping families together
/ Robert Bernstein. — 1st ed.
        p.   cm.
    Includes index.
    ISBN 1-56025-085-2 : $24.95 ($32.50 Can.). — ISBN
1-56025-086-0 (pbk.) : $12.95
        1. Parents & Friends of Lesbians and Gays. 2. Parents of
gays—United States—Attitudes. 3. Lesbians—United States—
Family relationships. 4. Gay men—United States—Family
relationships. I. Title.
HO75.B47   1995
306.874–dc20   95-1358
                                                           CIP

Printed in the United States of America

Distributed by Publishers Group West
4065 Hollis Street
Emeryville, CA 94608
(800) 788-3123

To Leo and Paulette

Contents

Acknowledgments

My agent, Frances Goldin, provided me with the initial motivation to write this book and guided the later development of many aspects of it. The encouragement of Neil Ortenberg of Thunder's Mouth Press has been important throughout. My daughter Sharon's critique of an early draft supplied insights that largely informed the book's eventual shape and substance. And much thanks go to my editor, Robert Weisser, for his craft, wisdom, humor, and patience.

My wife, Myrna, has been a full partner in our P-FLAG adventure: sharing the journey of discovery, assisting in interviews, offering penetrating observations, reviewing drafts, and imparting her trademark aura of calm and caring that makes all of my work possible.

Myrna and I are convinced that the ghost of Will Rogers watches over P-FLAG meetings: we have never met anyone there we didn't like. And I could not have written this book without the generous and spirited cooperation of scores of P-FLAG members. Many of these people are mentioned in the book; I wish I had the room to list them all. They have my everlasting thanks.

I have borrowed from two remarkable videos about families with gay members, and I am grateful to their producers. They are Dee Mosbacher and Frances Reid (*Straight from the Heart*, Woman Vision Video, 3145 Geary Boulevard, Box 421, San Francisco, CA 94118; 415-346-2336) and Pam Walton (*Gay Youth*, Wolfe Video, PO Box 64, Almaden, CA 95042; 408-268-6782).

Janet Lowenthal's manuscript suggestions were invaluable. And for the advice and information they furnished me, I am indebted to Dr. Robert Rosen, Bud Clark, Phyllis Naylor, Eric Marcus, Michael Lowenthal, Gregory King, and the P-FLAG national staff.

Foreword

We have long been a country that hates and fears homo-sexuals, so it is extremely painful for parents to cope with the discovery that one of their children is homo-sexual. They may be shocked, hurt, bewildered, or angry. Those who have suspected the truth for a long time may take the news with equanimity, but most parents will react with denial or terrible grief. Their children are well aware of this, and desperately try to keep the truth from them. These families are badly in need of help, but know not where to turn. This book will be a life raft! What Robert Bernstein documents is how other parents have handled the situation, the help they have found, and the success most of them have had keeping their families together.

Parents, Families and Friends of Lesbians and Gays (P-FLAG) was formed in 1973 to give that help. The first group met in 1973, and it became a national movement in 1981, and has been grow-ing ever since. I have for many years been an honorary director of the organization.

I am involved in this issue because I write a column of advice for teenagers, called *Ask Beth*. It is syndicated in newspapers across the country and on Prodigy, the on-line computer service. From the beginning, hundreds of thousands of gay and lesbian teenagers have written to me in search of help. I get letters from their par-ents, too. This is not surprising, since homosexual teens have more than their share of serious problems, and have found in me a sympathetic ear—or perhaps pen. Although none of my own four children is gay, I was not raised to hate or fear those who were.

Most adolescents have a lot of painful memories growing up, but I soon realized gay kids' problems were far more difficult to help, since they were almost without exception locked firmly in the closet. The letter that made me fully appreciate their terror was from a sophomore high school student in the 1960s. He wrote that he had been up on the roof of his house all night trying to find the courage to jump and end it all. "But, I am too chicken even to do that. Oh please, can't you help me?" In my column, I answered with the phone number of the Hetrick-Martin Institute for the Protection of Gay and Lesbian Youth in New York City. I have no way of knowing what happened. Like most troubled kids, he gave me no home address.

It was extremely frustrating then trying to find places to refer gay or lesbian kids for sympathetic and knowledgeable help. Fortunately, there are more now. I became aware of P-FLAG early on, and have cheered its growth through the years.

What comes clear in so many of the histories in *Straight Parents/ Gay Children* is that when families face the issue honestly, they are stronger for it. In story after story, this fact is repeated. The "closet," as Bernstein explains, is an instrument of oppression. Once children come out and can at last be honest with their parents and know that they are still loved, the truth *does* set them free.

BETH WINSHIP

Introduction

I have a gay son and that's all right with me. What is important is my son the person—his character, his generosity, his talents. His sex life is of no more importance to me than that of his heterosexual brothers and sisters, or of my close friends. I find I get hugged a bit more than was common among men when my generation was young, but since as many of today's male huggers seem to be straight as are gay, I'm not sure it's a consequence of having a gay son. The only other consequence that occurs to me from time to time is that he won't be the father of any grandchildren, which is a pity because he would be very talented as a parent.

If all the parents with gay relatives could comfortably say "I have a gay child (grandchild, sibling, niece, nephew, cousin, aunt, uncle)," this book would be unnecessary. But millions of parents cannot do this. Some of them are afraid of what others will say. Others are appalled that their children are gay. Still others are ashamed, imagining that something they did caused an effect they have been taught to consider sick and unnatural. And many more are simply unaware, because their gay sons and daughters are afraid to tell them.

Straight Parents/Gay Children can be a great comfort to these millions of parents. Through the collective experience of thousands of families, it reveals that, once over the threshold of misinformation and fear, parents can find liberation in the truth about homosexuality. And this liberation restores and strengthens the natural bonds of love and understanding they have with their sons and daughters.

Parents learn that it is not their children's choice to fall in love with members of their own sex. It is something over which they have no control. The farther scientists reach for answers, the greater the conviction that homosexuality is innate, predetermined, fixed. It is neither a defect of moral character nor a failure of will. Some people may consider it blasphemous to call homosexuality an act of God; let us then consider it an act of Nature. Efforts to change that nature, whether cruel or kind, are doomed to failure. Queen Victoria's opinion that women could not be homosexuals did not change any gay person's sexual preference at the beginning of the century. Neither did Nazi persecution at mid-century. Nor will the present attempts to curb the civil rights of gay people.

There is a great need for the comfort this book can bring to anguished parents by helping them find others like themselves. The most informed estimates place the number of gay Americans at about 15 million, and almost every gay person has relatives somewhere in this world. Theoretically, there may be 15 million siblings of gay children, 30 million parents, 60 million grandparents, and so on through other relations. Statistically, as much as half of all Americans have a reasonably direct stake in understanding homosexuality. Many do not know it because so many gay people keep their sexuality a secret. Many know it, but deny or suppress the truth. Others know it, and live in misery fearing the ostracism of society.

When a story about my good relations with my son, Ian, appeared in the New York Times, I received many letters from parents of gay children saying how the article helped them acknowledge the truth. One mother wrote that for years she had suspected her son's secret misery. She slipped the article under his bedroom door, and a few minutes later he came out—in both senses. There were other letters of greater pain, from young people whose parents had never accepted their homosexuality and who had disowned them.

Prejudice against homosexuality is deeply rooted in our culture because of religious and psychological legacies difficult to
unravel. As with any prejudice, this one runs counter to evidence.
President Clinton failed in his intention to repeal the ban on gays
in the military because the defense community considered it too
disruptive, although most people know that homosexuals have
always served, some with great distinction.

No one in this book is advocating special treatment for gay
people. What they are advocating is that gay Americans be treated decently so that their families need not fear to love them, and so
that millions of Americans need not fear disgrace, discrimination,
and physical assault for their sexual orientation. Relieving the
ostracism of gay Americans would strengthen family values, no
matter what the prevailing political climate may dictate.

Finally, on civil rights grounds, I don't think it can be put more
eloquently than Senator Barry Goldwater has done:

> The rights and liberties that our founding fathers wrote into
> the Declaration of Independence and the Constitution were meant
> for all people. . . . It is time that our nation realized that a signifi-
> cant portion of our society is today excluded and that laws need
> to be written and enforced to ensure that lesbians and gays are
> not discriminated against in employment, public accommoda-
> tions, and housing.

ROBERT MACNEIL

Keeping families together is the mission of P-FLAG. Our family values stress education, understanding, acceptance, and support, but most of all, *love*, thereby empowering our children—straight and gay— to lead happy and productive lives.

from a letter to the editor in the Colorado Springs *Independent*

1

◆

Rethinking the Unthinkable

My younger daughter, after years of denying to herself that she was gay,* ultimately told the truth to herself, her family, and her personal world. She is one of millions of Americans who increasingly are refusing to live lives of deception, to lie about an important aspect of who they are. And she has thereby led her family down new pathways of understanding.

Telling the truth can set psyches free. It can strengthen family bonds. It can make our society a healthier place. As young people struggle to understand their inner natures, and parents struggle to accept their children's sexuality, honesty and openness are healing ingredients. As society struggles against the sway of ignorance and prejudice, truth, coupled with regard for the dignity and individuality of others, is an indispensable weapon.

This is a book about truth-telling and respect for human differences. It is the story of some extraordinary individuals and a pioneering organization that have demonstrated those qualities' immense potential for good.

Yes, truth-telling can be rewarding. But it can also be difficult and risky. And it is rarely easy.

* Throughout the book, I have used the word *gay* in its generic sense to refer to both gay men and lesbians, as well as to those who identify as bisexual.

*   *   *

"How do you feel about having a gay son?"

The question was directed to Paul, sitting with ten or twelve others around a table in a large conference room in a local church. His wife Marie had just finished describing her response to their son John's revelation that he was homosexual. She had recounted a persistent, pervasive grief similar to what she had felt when her mother died five years earlier. Periodically, she had said, without warning, she was wracked by uncontrollable sobbing. As she spoke, the tears came again.

Across from Paul and Marie, Joan was recovering her composure after telling tearfully how her daughter had come out to her as a lesbian. "I can't imagine what I did wrong," she had said. "Maybe I should have dated more after my divorce, or had more men around the house . . . Maybe I shouldn't have let her play sports . . . Now I can't imagine what sort of terrible life she's going to have."

Paul had come reluctantly, at Marie's urging, and sat stiffly as she sobbed. Now the question to him hung in the air as he looked first at his wife and then turned to the questioner. His response was bitter: "Isn't everybody delighted to have a queer in the family?"

The responses of Paul, Marie, and Joan are typical of parents when they first learn they have a gay child. To most non-gay people, homosexuality is mysterious, embarrassing, and even downright disgusting. And the possibility that their own child might be gay is usually quite unthinkable to parents. Homosexuals, we've been conditioned to believe, are perverts, labeled as pathological by the medical profession, sinful by the churches, and criminal by the legal system. Although the term *homophobia* has only recently become part of our general vocabulary, the attitude it describes— an unreasonable fear and hatred of homosexuals and homosexuality—was simply part of the atmosphere in which we all grew up, part of the air we breathed, as it were. We could no more have avoided being homophobic than a medieval serf could have doubted the world was flat.

So it is not surprising that parents who learn they have a gay child typically feel a mixture of shock, disbelief, shame, and guilt. Nevertheless, there *is* another face to this picture. And I can personally testify that for parents of gay kids, that other face can be as bright and joyful as the one painted by conventional wisdom is bleak and frightening.

Paul, Marie, and Joan sought assistance from an organization called P-FLAG—Parents, Families and Friends of Lesbians and Gays—which among its other activities conducts support groups for distraught parents. There, parents of gay children can rethink the unthinkable, restore their sense of well-being, and reclaim the families they thought were irreparably shattered. Their initial negative feelings gradually shade into tolerance and then acceptance. And many move on to still another phase: impatience with the prejudice and stereotyping that relegates their loved ones to second-class citizenship. For P-FLAG does more than provide support groups. Through education and advocacy, it directly challenges the myths and irrational beliefs on which anti-gay sentiments are based. In effect, the P-FLAG experience is one of learning, heightened awareness, and personal growth. And for many it is a spur to speak out and tell the world what they have learned.

As parents, it turns out, we can learn a lot from our gay kids about such significant matters as personal integrity and respect for individual differences. Legions of us have come to terms with our children's homosexuality and discovered that our lives were not diminished but actually enriched by the process. In this way, P-FLAG functions as a sort of alchemist of the soul, converting bereaved parents into active celebrants of diversity. It leads us gently through the barbed thickets of misguided conventional wisdom and back to where we belong—at our children's sides. In its support groups, we can let our anguish hang out, secure in the empathy of those who have experienced the same sense of devastation and loss.

We can sense in others the healing qualities of time and understanding. And we soon become closer than ever to our children.

We learn that parents do not "cause" and our children for the most part do not "choose" their sexual orientation. We learn that the much-maligned "lifestyle" of the average gay person is about as lurid as our own, being centered on such mundane matters as job, family, friends, home, hobbies, and church. The gay community, it turns out, contains about the same proportion of saints and rascals as any other.

We learn that homosexuality is a lot like left-handedness: a minority but wholly natural and neutral trait which speaks not at all to character or morality. We come to appreciate the courage, sensitivity, and integrity demanded of those who manage, despite society's fierce antagonism, to say simply, "I am what I am."

We learn that the genesis of our distress with our children's gayness is neither our children nor ourselves. It is society's reluctance to renounce archaic myths, superstitions, and hatred. There is nothing "wrong" with our gay children.

But we can't help worrying about them.

For there is something very wrong with a society that irrationally denigrates and discriminates against them. A society that limits their job and housing opportunities. A society that drives gay youth to despair and suicide. A society that tacitly encourages the physical violence that is commonly their lot.

While gay teenagers face despair and death for lack of support and role models, the Supreme Court refuses to review a case approving the dismissal of a high school guidance counselor because she is bisexual. In Washington, D.C., two high school students mutilate a gay man in an effort to castrate him—and are granted probation by an obviously sympathetic judge. In Florida, a judge jokingly asks a prosecuting attorney, "That's a crime now, to beat up a homosexual?" When told, "Yes, sir, and it's also a crime to kill them," he notes, "Times have really changed." In Dallas, a judge is reelected by overwhelming vote after righteously announcing he would give the lightest possible sentence to a hooligan who gunned down, gangster-style, two young gay men.

Gay-bashing appears to serve much the same function lynching once did: controlling a despised minority through terror. Most anti-gay violence is not prosecuted, if for no other reason than that the victims do not dare file charges; the publicity could cost them their jobs and their homes. Discrimination based on sexual orientation—firing or evicting an employee or tenant simply because he or she is gay—is protected by the laws of all but eight states and a handful of municipalities. And in most states, gay people can be jailed for physically expressing their love in relationships as stable as those of the most devoted heterosexual couples.

Slowly, very slowly, attitudes are changing. Honesty and openness are gaining in fashion. Gays are recognizing the liberating force of coming out of the closet. Their families and friends are learning to discern between the realities and myths of homosexuality, and to speak out about their newfound truths.

In these pages, you'll meet some parents who are helping lead the way, including the following:

- The highly regarded police chief of Portland, Oregon, who marched in gay pride parades alongside his lesbian daughter, who was one of his own officers.
- Celebrities such as television journalist Robert MacNeil, former Senator Barry Goldwater, and Senator Claiborne Pell, who are joining the ranks of openly supportive parents of gay children.
- An orthopedic surgeon, fitness buff, and national senior power lifting champion who said, "I wish I could be as good a man as my son"—a former "Top Gun" being drummed out of the service because he is gay.
- A mild-mannered schoolteacher who is acknowledged as the first parent to carry a sign rallying other parents to the support of their gay kids.

- A Methodist bishop who simply "knew" that if his own son was gay, the stereotypes had to be wrong, and who has campaigned for decades for increased tolerance within his denomination.
- A Jewish immigrant whose family was decimated by the Holocaust, but who lived to speak—as the mother of a gay child—at the inauguration of the United States Holocaust Memorial Museum on behalf of gay Holocaust victims.

For many of us, P-FLAG has provided a crucial assist in reaching a fuller appreciation of human complexity. I envision the organization as the tip of an iceberg, the visible bit of a potentially millions-strong constituency capable of massive positive social change. By reasonable estimate, the number of gay, lesbian, and bisexual Americans is probably about fifteen million. The number of non-gay people who might be expected to be their natural allies—their parents, siblings, cousins, aunts, uncles, grandparents, and close friends—is therefore enormous.

Many of these friends and relatives remain caught up in society's prevailing mood of intolerance. But I am convinced that many of them are now silent simply because they are unaware that their silence helps perpetuate the oppression of those they love. They do not realize that they themselves have the power to end that injustice by speaking out against it.

I believe that the parents, families, and friends of gays will be in the vanguard of any meaningful breakthrough to the soul of America. We speak to the mainstream *from* the mainstream. We wield the clout of sheer numbers. We are—potentially—a powerful army for social good. But our ranks are now missing millions of troops who do not realize how desperately they are needed in the trenches.

2

♦

Growing Up Gay

Some people would rather die than let their parents know they are gay.

Leonard Jenkins was fourteen when he was saved by another student who found him hanging by his neck from a rafter in an Akron high school storage building. After the incident, the school counselor told Leonard's mother, Rada, that he would "rather his kid came home with cancer" than be gay.

A couple I met at a support group told a similar tale. Speaking through her tears, the mother recounted how, after being unable to reach their thirty-year-old son by telephone, they drove to his apartment house and prevailed upon the superintendent to unlock their son's door. They found him near death from an overdose of sleeping pills, and got him to a hospital in time. There, he later revealed to them that he was gay.

First-person accounts of growing up gay almost always include periods of black despair and suicidal thoughts. In fact, gay teenagers do commit suicide in disproportionately high numbers, and legions of them self-destruct more indirectly through the avenues of substance abuse or promiscuity. Father Robert Nugent, a priest with a ministry to gay Catholics, has summed it up eloquently: "To grow up gay in a society carrying the burden of being classified 'sick' by the medical profession, 'criminal' by the legal system, and 'sinful' by popular religious beliefs is one that few of us could bear without severe and permanent emotional damage."

Most members of minority groups can look to their own families for understanding, support, guidance, and role modeling. "You're a fine human being," the old black man tells his granddaughter on the television series *I'll Fly Away*. "You're as good as anyone else and don't you ever let *anyone* tell you different." But gay kids rarely hear that kind of support. John Favretto, who grew up gay in Bethesda, Maryland, puts it succinctly: "We can't come home crying and say, 'The straight kids made fun of me at school today.'" To be young and gay is often to be desperately alone.

Much of the energy of gay adolescents goes into maintaining a web of deception about their sexual orientation. They perceive, correctly, that candor could bring not only rejection by family and friends, but also physical jeopardy. For coming out publicly is an act of high courage. It is, among other things, a decision to be on guard for the rest of your life.

For Tony, a seventeen-year-old Arizonan, coming out meant having a pole smashed in his face by a classmate screaming "Fag." When he came to, he found his boyfriend lying near him with two broken ribs and a concussion. Tony later dropped out of school because of the abuse he faced every day. (The Gay and Lesbian Task Force has estimated that 28 percent of gay adolescents do likewise.)

A sixteen-year-old boy in northern California was brutally kicked in the stomach by schoolmates. For days, the pain was intense, but he could tell his mother only that he was "just feeling sick"—he was not yet out at home. He subsequently swallowed a bottle of muscle relaxants in a suicide attempt.

Growing up in Lafayette, Louisiana, Kevyn Aucoin was taunted and assaulted by schoolmates for his "sissy" interests and mannerisms. He thought often of killing himself; but he couldn't be certain that local anti-gay toughs wouldn't beat him to it. After two boys in a pickup truck tried to run him over, he dropped out of high school and moved to Baton Rouge. There, he was beaten by a security guard and undercover detectives at a store when he was applying for work. He fled to New York.

Kevyn's story, unlike that of so many others, has a happy ending. After years of struggling in the Big Apple, he became a lion of the fashion industry: a makeup artist whose work was the first ever to be featured on nine consecutive *Vogue* covers, and a close friend of some of the biggest stars of the entertainment and fashion worlds. "I guess there was one shred of dignity that kept me hanging on," he says. "One shred of belief that I was a human being." But he couldn't forget other youngsters growing up gay in Louisiana, "with nobody to help them," and after squaring his gayness with his parents, he persuaded them to launch a P-FLAG chapter in Lafayette.

Everywhere gay kids turn, they hear the same message: "You are despicable." And their typical assumption that their family is an unlikely source of support is probably correct. A June 1994 story in the *New York Times* told of a gay boy whose arm was deeply lacerated because his father had thrown him through a glass door; it told of another whose face was badly scarred because his mother had burned him so he "would not be attractive to other men." These of course are extreme examples. But they reflect a parental negativity endemic to society.

More than a quarter of all gay and lesbian youth who come out to their parents are actually ejected from their homes, according to George Ayala, associate executive director of New York City's Hetrick-Martin Institute, which provides social services, education, and advocacy for gay and lesbian adolescents. Ayala says that teenagers thrown out of their homes by their parents turn up daily on the Institute's doorstep, and claims that 40 to 50 percent of all homeless youth in New York City are gay or lesbian.

To Lyn, who grew up in southern California, expulsion from her family home might have been preferable to what did happen. She says her mother had her locked up in a mental hospital. There, she says, she was subjected to "aversion therapy" consisting of, among other horrors, being given medication to nauseate her and then being shown pornographic pictures of girls. As a crowning irony, her mother sent her a get-well card!

And as Matthew tells it, his parents seemed to compete to see which could be more cruel.

Matthew grew up in the Midwest, and he says that at sixteen he was "your basic over-achiever." A student body officer and a member of the National Honor Society, he had accelerated his courses so he could graduate as a junior and spend the next year as an exchange student abroad.

Then, a few months before graduation, he told his brother he was gay. The next day, his brother told their mother, whose first reaction was to tell Matthew he was "just doing this to get attention." She canceled his plans for the year abroad, then tried to find a psychiatrist who would try to "cure" him. (She failed to find one who would see him on those terms.) Finally, she banished Matthew from her house, sending him to live with his father, from whom she was divorced. This arrangement lasted just one week before his father declared it "his duty as a God-fearing American citizen" not to allow homosexuality in his household.

Matthew told me that his father picked him up and threw him out the door of the house, and then came out and attacked him. He recalled his father yelling, "I brought you into this world, I can take you out!" as the two struggled. Matthew's father soon overcame him, and locked his neck in a leghold so tight that he couldn't breathe—much less voice the apology his father was demanding. "I would have said anything at that point just to get him off me," Matthew said. But he passed out, thinking he would never wake up. When he did, he was being carried into the house by his grandmother and his boyfriend, who had witnessed the horrible scene. He immediately packed his belongings, left his father's home, and hasn't seen his parents since.

*   *   *

Ironically, even when parents are likely to be supportive, the pervasive climate of intolerance often deters youngsters from seeking parental help. Consider what happened to Michael Larson.

Michael knew from age nine that he was gay but feared to tell anyone, particularly his devoutly religious parents, Bonnie and John. But when he was twenty, suicidal thoughts led him to confide in an Episcopal priest, and the priest recommended an organization called Regeneration, which promised to help him "change" his orientation. That didn't work, and Michael was wracked by shame over what he felt was a terrible character flaw. He sought solace in furtive sex and was arrested in a police stakeout of a public park. In desperation, he turned to his last hope. He called home and confessed all to his parents.

To Michael's surprise, they told him that while they didn't understand, they loved and accepted him; if he was gay, they would learn what they needed to know about that. Thus, it was at home that Michael found true regeneration. Within a few years, openly gay, he was in a committed relationship and running his own business in Charlotte, North Carolina. And his parents kept their promise to learn what they needed to know about gayness. Bonnie Larson is now the director of the four-state P-FLAG region that encompasses her Pittsburgh home.

In an ideal world, the Larsons' response to their son would be the model. But in our world, even when parents don't shun their gay children, their ingrained prejudices often lead them to make spontaneous, hurtful comments. At support group meetings, young people frequently tell of parents crying, "How could you do this to me?" As if it is the parents who have been victimized. As if their children would purposely relinquish their claim to mainstream respect and invite a lifetime of stigma, discrimination, and physical danger as a sort of selfish, rebellious frolic.

Why are parents so ill-equipped to handle the news? A treasure of P-FLAG tradition—a picture of the organization's founding mother, Jeanne Manford, marching beside her son Morty in New York's 1972 gay pride parade—suggests part of the answer. In the foreground, Manford is carrying a hand-lettered sign saying, "Parents of Gays Unite in Support for Our Children." (See Chapter 4.) Marching behind her is Dr. Benjamin Spock, child-rearing guru to generations of American parents.

The irony of this tableau is pointed out by Robb Forman Dew, prize-winning novelist and active New Hampshire P-FLAGger, in *The Family Heart*, her moving memoir about her son's coming out. She writes that her son first realized that he was "different" by the age of two or three, and notes that 30 percent of all teenage suicides result from the despair of gay and lesbian children. Nevertheless, she laments that neither Spock nor his fellow wizard of parenting, T. Berry Brazleton, ever offered her a hint of the significant truth "that parents' assumptions of the heterosexuality of their sons or daughters begin at birth and are a threat to their children's lives."

Rare is the doctor or nurse who discusses this matter with young parents. Nor do families get much-needed information from schools. Teachers, counselors, and sex-education courses, in theory, could help fill the void of ignorance for children as well as parents. Typically, however, conservative activists roll out the heavy cannons at the slightest threat of such enlightenment in public schools. Invoking "family values" and God, but often relying on archaic superstition and vicious rhetoric, they cow school boards and school officials into heeding their most preposterous statements. An example is a wild-eyed warning from the dean of a state university in the Southwest: "Since the homosexuals cannot reproduce, they must out of necessity recruit . . . my children and grandchildren and yours." As a result, sex education courses are outlawed or reduced to trivia. Potentially helpful books are banned or their access limited in school and other public libraries. Teachers and counselors, fearful for their positions, dare not even speak in tolerant terms much less show support for their frightened, besieged gay students.

The ignorance of many Americans and their apparent determination to stay that way were strikingly demonstrated by a national flap that arose in 1993 over the comic strip "For Better or for Worse." Scores of newspapers across the country actually refused to run a four-week episode of the strip in which a teenager comes out to his best friend and his parents. A summary of the episode strikingly reveals the down-home warmth and common sense of which, thanks to censorship, hundreds of thousands of American newspaper readers were deprived.

The sequence involved an ordinary seventeen-year-old, Lawrence Poirier, who tells his friend Mike that he is gay. Mike initially has some difficulty with the news, but the boys' friendship prevails. However, when Lawrence tells his parents, they grow hysterical. Lawrence's mother demonstrates a series of reactions commonly seen in P-FLAG support meetings:

- Disbelief: "I don't believe you." And, "It's a phase. You'll pass through it."
- Self-blame: "It's my fault. I was too protective. I should have pushed you harder." (To Lawrence's protestation that she is not to blame, she shouts, "I have to blame somebody!")
- Denial: "You are not gay! You are *not*."
- Finally, anger and desperation, as she calls for her husband: "TALK SOME SENSE INTO HIM!!!"

Lawrence's father instead kicks him out of the house, saying, "If that's the life you've chosen, I don't want you under this roof! . . . Go wherever 'your kind' hangs out!!!"

Later, repenting, the mother asks Mike to look for Lawrence. Mike finds his friend in an all-night diner, but Lawrence says, "Leave me alone. You can't help me. I'm sick." Mike says, "You're not sick, man. Trust me. I'm more open-minded than you think." "Believe me," says Lawrence, "after 11 jelly doughnuts and 6 coffees I'm sick."

The relieved parents welcome Lawrence home. "I'm not going

to judge you," his father says. "As long as you're a good man and a kind man I'll respect you. As for the rest, what will be will be, que sera sera." (The family later names their new puppy "Sera.") The warmth of the two boys' families ultimately triumphs over the initial shock of Lawrence's coming out.

The basic theme of the episode was that families can pull together and learn to accept even when they don't understand. But the rationale for censorship offered by the editor of one newspaper reveals much of society's thoughtless misunderstanding on the subject. His newspaper, the editor wrote, was merely drawing the line "between live-and-let-live tolerance and love-me-love-my-lifestyle advocacy." Thus, he said, the decision merely supported Americans' general refusal "to grant full social approval to homosexual lifestyles."

The strip had said nothing about lifestyles of any kind. It gave no indication that Lawrence even had a boyfriend, much less that he had had homosexual relations. Rather, it simply dealt with an inner experience—the hormonal reality that he was attracted to men rather than to women. And what the strip did say—for example, that the parents did not rule out the possibility that their son could be both gay and "a good man and a kind man"—had nothing to do with advocacy of any sort. It might well, however, have saved the lives of some despairing young readers.

This uproar over a comic strip demonstrates how gay people have been demonized—conceived as weird, alien creatures who are wholly different from the rest of us plain folk. Thus, an editor can look at an episode portraying a young man's emotions and see it as endorsing some sort of subversive lifestyle. An otherwise loving father, as in the strip itself, can order his son to go "wherever 'your kind' hangs out." The immense cruelty of these attitudes is reflected in the son's poignant response, as he cries out in the darkness outside the house, "What do you mean 'my kind.' My name is Lawrence Poirier—and I live *here*!!!"

Ostrich-like, society insistently refuses to accept the comic

strip's common-sense approach to homosexuality. Instead, it tacitly promotes the grief, despair, dissolution, and death bred by
myth and superstition. The misery will continue until educators,
pediatricians, and politicians begin speaking out about what many
of them know but fear to say: that there will always be a significant
minority of our children who are gay, no matter what anybody
says or does. Ideally, they would also say what Dr. Spock's presence at that 1972 march suggests he surely must have long known
—that children can be both gay and okay.

Unfortunately, that ideal may be far off. Even as I write,
Congress threatens to inscribe homophobia as a uniform national educational standard.

In 1994, a conservative electoral wave brought to Congress a
Republican majority pledged to what its leaders called "Contract
with America." The Contract itself did not mention homosexuality,
but many of its signers endorsed a plan that would in effect put
out a contract on the lives of innocent gay youth. The potential
killer was an amendment to an appropriations bill, sidetracked in
the prior Congress, but set to be reintroduced by Representative
Mel Hancock of Missouri. It would deny federal funds to schools
that suggest in any manner that homosexuality is "a positive
lifestyle alternative"; its effect would be to bar most of the nation's
schools from providing one iota of emotional support—most
explicitly including kind words—to maligned and already-despair-
ing gay students. "If your school treats gay kids decently, you lose
federal money," Representative Barney Frank of Massachusetts
summed up.

This is the social environment—a hostile wilderness dotted with
emotional land mines—in which my daughter Bobbi had to come
to grips with her gayness. That she seems to have emerged relatively unscathed without the aid of either parental or community
support is a tribute both to her courage and her good fortune. An
overriding regret for me—and for many other P-FLAG parents—

is that her mother, stepmother, and I could not help her when she needed us most. I like to think that we could have spared her years of inner terror and doubt; that we would have given her the time and emotional space to discover for herself, without fear or panic, the nature of her sexual identity; that we would have assured her that whatever her orientation might be, it would never diminish either her worth as a person or our own love for her.

I like to think this would have been the case, but I cannot be totally confident of it. For when Bobbi was a teenager struggling to find her place in the world, her mother, stepmother, and I were still full-fledged members of the homophobic mainstream. Could we have responded with understanding, accepting, and patience? I don't know, and the answer is now irrelevant. Only after years of her lonely inner struggle with her identity would she describe it to us.

Her principal weapon in her struggle to quell her unwanted feelings was denial. Before high school, she had fleeting crushes on other girls, but gave them no particular thought. Then, one day in high school, she found herself aroused by another girl. She thought, "She's really sexy," but the feeling was unacceptable. "You didn't think that," she told herself. "Forget that." And for the most part, she did manage to ignore and repress such feelings. But the occasional thought that she might be gay triggered spasms of terror.

Bright, talented, extroverted, and a standout athlete, Bobbi made friends easily. She dated a number of boys, and formed lasting (but passionless) friendships with at least two of them. Dating reinforced her denial and seemed to make the threat of her deeper stirrings more remote. By her senior year, she was aware that she wanted a boyfriend so that other people wouldn't think she was gay, but she was still denying the possibility to herself. To maintain her belief, she had to resort to some off-beat logic: since her attraction to women was different from her attraction to men, the former was not sexual and therefore did not mean she was gay. But mental gymnastics would not long stem the mounting inner pressures.

After high school, she enrolled at Stanford, where she met a number of openly homosexual students in a relatively gay-friendly climate. Nevertheless, her self-denial and its accompanying anxiety continued to grow during her first year. Secretly, she was deeply in love with her roommate, and that terrified her. She even turned to religion, until then a matter of indifference to her. Her religious background had been haphazard: she had attended occasional Protestant services with her mother, and had sometimes come to my Unitarian church when staying with me. Now, however, she seriously considered embracing Catholicism. She thought that if she went to church often enough, if she prayed hard enough, perhaps her dreaded feelings would go away. Three or four times a day, she intoned the standard Hail Mary and Lord's Prayer, capped by the plaint, "Please, God, don't let me be gay." Only later would she learn that such frantic pleas to God are common among gay adolescents.

As she strained to prove to herself that she was "normal," Bobbi continued to date young men. Early in her sophomore year, she began to see Michael, a handsome, charming classmate. When she came home for Christmas vacation and people asked about Michael, she heard herself describing someone she clearly thought was wonderful. She told her friends, in all sincerity, that he was probably the most brilliant and talented person she had ever met—"And yeah, he's really cute."

Everybody assumed she was in love. But during that vacation, she met Sasha, whom she knew to be lesbian and whom she thought was a "dashingly beautiful woman." They spent some time together, did a lot of talking, and a close friendship bloomed. Bobbi found herself thinking more and more about Sasha.

On the plane back to school, she realized that she was dreading seeing Michael, and at first wondered why. Then suddenly, the likelihood she was gay burst through her wall of denial and into her consciousness.

She wrote to Sasha, baring her distress, and got back ten pages of sound advice: If you're gay that's fine, or if you're not, that's fine; but if you are, and really care about Michael, then you should be fair and release him. Bobbi accepted the wisdom. The news might hurt Michael for a while, but he was a good friend and she owed him honesty. He would get over it and find somebody who could love him the way he needed to be loved.

So she went to Michael's room and sat on the floor, her back to him as he sat on the edge of a chair, to tell him all. But for some minutes, she could only mumble incoherently. (Michael later said that the severity of her distress had led him to believe she was trying to tell him either that she was dying or sleeping with his best friend.) Finally, she spit it out: "Michael, I think I might be gay."

Michael was silent for what seemed to Bobbi an eternity. Then he took her hand and said, "I know this is a hard time for you. I want you to know that whatever you ultimately decide, I'm here for you." At that, Bobbi burst into tears, they hugged, and they talked until four in the morning.

Now, with no secrets between them, their friendship grew. Sometimes they would even sleep together, chastely, in each other's arms, just because it was so comfortable. Sasha came to visit Bobbi, and Michael spent pleasant hours with the two of them.

Bobbi did not immediately come out to all of her friends. So, ironically, the relaxed affability between Bobbi and Michael and their open affection led many on campus to assume they were an item. But of course Michael wanted to see other women, and one of them was a friend of Bobbi's. When Michael approached her, the friend was indignant: "How can you do this to Bobbi!" To rescue Michael, Bobbi was forced to come out to her friend sooner than she otherwise would have.

Soon, she had told all her friends. Spontaneously—almost magically—the oppression and terror so long her constant companions evaporated. But one set of anxieties was replaced by another. Life as an openly lesbian woman presented new challenges. Among the first was coming out to her family.

3

♦

Digesting the News

In the Broadway play *Twilight of the Golds*, the mother of a gay son tells him, "I must have dressed you funny. Or, I don't know, if only I hadn't taken your temperature that way."

This line inevitably draws one of the heartiest laughs of the evening. Clearly, theatergoers intuitively understand the nature of the trauma that mothers typically experience when they learn they have a gay child. Like the reflection in a fun-house mirror, the play's burlesque image is backed by a solid reality: parents of gay kids often suffer outrageous guilt.

But guilt is just one of a range of inner torments a child's coming out may arouse in parents. Many parents pass through a process quite similar to mourning the loss of a family member. In fact, they do experience a type of death—that of a set of important parental images and expectations, including visions of grandchildren and of a respectable and respected future for the child. In the shock of the parents' first reaction, the child of their cherished images seems no longer to exist.

Healing, as after an actual death, proceeds at different paces for different people, and is marked by disbelief, denial, grief, and anger, and ending, for most, in acceptance. But unlike the death of a loved one, this trauma can't be freely shared. Friends and neighbors don't bear food and solace to the family hearth. (God forbid they should even know!) Society provides no comforting rituals, no funerals or wakes.

Why are we so disturbed by homosexuality? The causes are complex. Part of the answer is simply the ageless human distrust of those who are "different," the same reaction that seems to underlie so much prejudice against those of different race, gender, and so on. But this difference has to do with sex, and that's an aspect of human nature that has generated more taboos, confusion, fears, and repression than any other.

So the emotional pressure-cooker in this instance projects some unusually vicious images, for which "deviant," "pervert," and "pedophile" are some of the generally accepted labels. And once programmed, as with other cultural prejudices, these images are reinforced by daily input from ordinary conversation, jokes, and the media. The drumbeat of negativity, moreover, creates the perception that sex is the defining aspect of homosexuals. They are not people who work, worship, tend their gardens, love their families, shop for groceries. They are sex-obsessed "sodomites."

Homosexuality also threatens traditional gender roles. So gay men are ridiculed as "pansies," too effeminate to be respected as "real" men. Lesbians are seen as man-hating "bull dykes," too unfeeling to assume their "proper" roles of dependency on men. And "traditional family values" becomes a catch-phrase sufficient in itself to convey the supposed social threat of homosexuality. For the truly traditional family is of course one in which gender roles are clear: male as head of the clan, female as servile homemaker.

All of this psychic unrest rationalizes handily into an unexamined assumption that gay people are sick or sinful or both. (See Chapter 5.) So it is hardly surprising that a child's coming out can be such a devastating blow to the unsuspecting parent.

When Bobbi came out to her family, her mother Carol and I had been divorced for some years. Carol's reaction was largely typical. When Bobbi spoke the fateful words, "I'm gay," Carol first tried to pass it off as a joke. "That's not funny," she said. When she realized Bobbi was serious, she said Bobbi must be mistaken: "You haven't really given boys a try." Then guilt and grief descended upon her, and became her overriding emotions for the next several months.

Like the mother in *Twilight of the Golds,* Carol castigated herself with a litany of self-blame. She had not been caring enough. She shouldn't have let Bobbi play sports. She should have remarried so that Bobbi would always have had "a man around the house." (Carol and I separated when Bobbi was seven.) She shouldn't have allowed Bobbi to attend a "liberal" college. She shouldn't have agreed to giving Bobbi a name that sounds like a boy's. Or even (as Bobbi insists Carol once remarked) she shouldn't have married someone shorter than herself.

Out of the blue, she would be overcome by despondency and break into tears, even when she hadn't been thinking of Bobbi. She envisioned a life of loneliness and desolation for her daughter. And she found herself largely unable to share her anguish with friends.

I had the good fortune to be spared much of the grief Carol was experiencing. As a young man, my attitude toward homosexuality was shamefully hateful. I remember I was proud to be friends with a college fraternity brother who was a gay-basher. A tall, muscular boy, though ordinarily of easygoing nature, he was driven by some compelling malice to attack the few open homosexuals he encountered in off-campus night spots. His high moral dudgeon and its savage expression were greatly admired by the "brothers." And I was among the admirers.

But events of the intervening years softened my harsh undergraduate views. I sympathized with the goals of the movements for civil rights of African Americans, women, and the disabled; and I began to wonder whether gays, like other minority groups, were despised largely out of irrational prejudice. I had taken my first steps as a "recovering homophobe." Most importantly, though, I had begun to suspect, when Bobbi was quite young, that she might be gay.

Ironically, my suspicions arose from stereotypical thinking triggered by Bobbi's "boyish" mannerisms and "tomboy" interests. Even when quite small, for example, she was intensely competitive in sports. My suspicions took root when she was only eight or nine years old—at least ten years before she was to admit to herself that she was gay, and perhaps before she had experienced any sexual stirrings whatever. But this stereotypical thinking actually served me well—at least I was *thinking* about a matter that forced me to confront my ingrained unease over homosexuality.

At first I was dismayed by the thought that my darling little girl might be one of "them." (I had no such concerns, for similarly stereotypical reasons, about my equally darling but more "feminine" older daughter, Sharon.) I was able to express my fears to Myrna, to whom I was then engaged; and we discussed the matter often in ensuing years. Bits of genuine evidence did emerge, such as Bobbi's utter lack of adolescent excitement toward the attractive boys she dated as a teenager. By the time of her ultimate disclosure, we were sufficiently prepared to avoid panic or shout disapproval. We were far from understanding all the personal and social ramifications of Bobbi's act. But at least we could assure her that her gayness did not diminish our love for her.

Myrna and I were fortunate. We had adjusted gradually to information that usually strikes unwary parents with mind-blowing impact. We had acknowledged the reality that whether gay or not, Bobbi would remain the same accomplished and gracious young woman who, like my other daughter and Myrna's two sons, made us proud. We now simply had an additional piece of information about Bobbi. To be sure, it was information that in our moral bookkeeping we at first automatically entered in the debit column. But we didn't expect any of our children to be perfect. And if being gay was to us a fairly substantial liability—well,

Bobbi's numerous assets still, for us, struck a clear balance in the black.

Bobbi came out to Myrna and me on a summer evening in 1987, between her sophomore and junior years at Stanford. She was shocked by our lack of surprise or distress. But if we were not surprised, we were nevertheless enlightened. Her story afforded us our first glimpse into the extraordinary process of coming out. (The phrase of course is shorthand for "coming out of the closet," and refers to the acknowledgment of one's same-sex orientation to oneself and to others.) We began to realize that it involves much more than mere declaration; rather, it is an inner dynamic, a journey of struggle and growth. It is a profound human experience, reflecting the ageless human striving for personal integrity. It is the effort to find and embrace one's authentic self—to say, "I am what I am, and that's okay"—in the face of a hostile society that inundates gay youth with shame. In effect, coming out represents liberation from hand-me-down "truths"—the powerful "shoulds" and "must nots" of encrusted social norms—that, unexamined, can produce a type of emotional bondage.

Myrna and I did not then realize the full impact Bobbi's coming out would have on our own lives. But we were fascinated and impressed by the story she told us that night—and in particular by the tender maturity of her relationship with Michael.

Afterward, I lay in bed processing what Bobbi had told us. My respect for my daughter was enhanced by the events she had related. If her homosexuality reflected something "wrong" with her, I thought, there was nevertheless something right about the way she was dealing with it. I could only applaud her rigorous honesty with herself and with those to whom she was close, such as Michael and her own family.

I thought also about the years through which Bobbi had suffered, terrified and alone because of feelings she dared not share with anyone else, least of all her parents. It was my first real inkling of the tortuous obstacle course gay kids have to negotiate without the support society automatically provides for others. I thought about growing up under those circumstances—without parents, peers, role models, or supportive teachers to provide the essential feedback that says, "You're all right." And, in the dark, I sobbed.

One day shortly after Bobbi's coming out, Carol and I had lunch. She was still in shock, envisioning a bleak, loveless life for Bobbi. I didn't think that that had to be the case, but I had no real evidence to support my assurances. However, I did come up with an idea that not only helped Carol adjust but set my own life on a new course of discovery and enrichment.

I recalled having seen notices in my church bulletin about meetings of a group called Parents and Friends of Lesbians and Gays. (Families wasn't added to P-FLAG's name until 1993.) In my ignorance, I told Carol it was part of the church program; only later did I learn that P-FLAG was an international organization whose local chapter just happened to meet in our church. I said that Myrna and I would accompany Carol if she wanted to go to a meeting. Carol agreed.

So it was that a few weeks later, my wife, my ex-wife, and I attended our first P-FLAG meeting. Like the evening of Bobbi's coming out, the meeting for me proved to be a moving experience that hinted at new horizons of awareness.

The facilitator of the meeting, Paulette Goodman, was a prototypical grandmother, short and full-bodied, with kindly eyes smiling through thick rimless eyeglasses. She spoke with a mild French accent in soft tones that were nonetheless precise and compelling. She would later become widely known during her four-year tenure as P-FLAG's national president, when her influence would extend into the White House itself. (Her story is told in Chapter 10.) At the moment, as she informed the group, she was both the local chapter president and Mid-Atlantic regional director of P-FLAG.

She described the organization as dedicated to the support and education of parents, but also to helping create a better society for those she referred to as "our gay loved ones."

For some reason, I found the latter phrase particularly compelling. It suggested that at P-FLAG, the term *gay* would not be used to connote perversion and deviance, but to refer to precious, valued family members. It suggested there were numerous others with gay children like Bobbi, whom they considered to be fine, worthwhile human beings.

The group included five or six gay and lesbian people. One was a handsome young man, tall, blond, blue-eyed—in appearance and manner a young woman's classic heartthrob. Bob worked as a bank teller and was majoring in finance as a part-time university student; he wanted to come out to his Midwestern parents but feared their reaction, particularly his father's.

Lisa was a schoolteacher, and in a committed relationship with a young woman with whom she lived. She loved her job, but was terrified that school authorities might discover she was a lesbian. She had come out to her parents some months earlier. So far, she said, they were "not very good about it"; and she was hoping to persuade them to attend a P-FLAG meeting near their home in the South.

Pete, a professional who would become a fond friend of ours, told us he had been married and had an eight-year-old daughter. He and his wife had divorced when he could no longer deny his gayness to himself or her, but he had maintained a close relationship with his daughter. At the moment, she was at the zoo with Pete's life companion, a lawyer, whom she fondly called "Uncle Steve"; she was staying with Pete and Steve for the weekend, as she did regularly under Pete's visitation arrangements. (When the meeting was over, we met Steve and the happy little girl, when they arrived to pick up her father.) Pete attended P-FLAG meetings, he said, to help assure parents that their gay sons could live stable, happy lives.

Among the parents were Veronica and Jerry Colfer, both seventy-eight, who like us were attending their first meeting. They had known for fourteen years that their son was gay and had long since come to full acceptance. Nevertheless, as devout Catholics, they had fearfully refrained from discussing the matter with friends or fellow parishioners. After years of closeted discomfort, they took obvious relief in being able to speak freely about their love for their son Paul and his lover Tom. They were there in part because the pressure to reveal their situation to others had increased: Tom had AIDS. The Colfers referred to Tom as their "son-in-love," a term fondly used (with its counterpart "daughter-in-love") by P-FLAG parents.

When it was her turn to speak, Carol expressed her misgivings at some length, weeping openly at one point. Gently, Paulette and others assured her that her feelings were common to "new parents" (another common P-FLAG term). Their empathy and understanding provided immediate relief, and her "recovery" moved rapidly from that point.

I had long taken a certain pride in being what I considered progressive and open-minded. But as I listened to the young gay people, I could not deny my sense of surprise that they seemed not to fit the stereotypes in my mind. And as I listened to Paulette and some of the "old parents," I realized how ignorant I was of a matter on which I no longer had any right to be uninformed.

Paulette might have been addressing me when she gently but firmly corrected a mother who suggested her gay son was not normal. Just because they comprise a minority, Paulette said, homosexual people are no less normal than other minorities, such as, for example, those who are left-handed. Societies throughout history have had approximately the same proportion of homosexual persons, she said; some of the most illustrious figures of history have been gay, and some cultures, such as Native Americans, have reserved special places of honor for their gay members.

I was moved by what I was hearing. Perhaps after all, I thought, there was nothing wrong with the daughter I respected so deeply. Perhaps *whom* she loved was not as important as the fact that she was capable of loving. Perhaps "gay loved one" was not necessarily an oxymoron.

Among her announcements that day, Paulette told us of a national gay and lesbian march on Washington scheduled for some weeks later. Neither Carol nor I had ever taken part in any sort of political demonstration. But we both lived in the suburbs of Washington and decided to go, since it seemed a relatively simple way of demonstrating support for Bobbi (who was already back at Stanford).

Myrna decided not to accompany us. Keenly aware of the prevalence of anti-gay sentiments, Myrna was beset by scary visions of ugly confrontations created by parade protesters. So she wished Carol and me well—but no thanks, she'd stay home. After hearing about our experience, she regretted her decision, and now enjoys marching with P-FLAG in similar parades.

October 11, 1987, was a crisp, sunny day in the nation's capital. Carol and I stood for more than an hour with our relatively tiny delegation of parents—a grizzled crew of maybe 150, virtually lost in a sea of some 600,000 mostly young people thronging Memorial Mall. But we were surprised to see banners indicating that parents had come from as far away as California, Colorado, and Washington state. Some carried signs with simple messages of support, such as "We love our gay and lesbian children." Finally, at a signal from parade marshals, we began a slow march through the Ellipse and onto Seventeenth Street. From there the throng would walk the short block to Pennsylvania Avenue and turn right, past the White House and toward Capitol Hill.

We hadn't taken more than twenty-five steps when we began to hear a low rumble that, to Carol and me, seemed ominous. Already a little edgy in this unfamiliar setting, we glanced at each other apprehensively. Gay rights marches, after all, were for us hardly common fare. Our confusion and unease heightened as the sound grew in volume.

Then, as we looked around us, we understood what we were hearing. The rumble was actually a growing roar of welcome from the massive throng, directed to our little band! It crescendoed into a deafening ovation that followed us up Seventeenth Street and all the way along Pennsylvania Avenue. For us, the march became a blur of excited faces, shouting voices, and waves of wild applause. Many of the faces were streaked with tears. Youths ran sobbing from the curbside to hug us, crying, "I wish my parents were here." Others with cameras swarmed about us, eager to preserve the memory of our symbolic presence.

Plainly, the thunder and the tears were welling up out of a vast void in the hearts of these young people. By their tumultuous ovation, they were telling us how profoundly they longed for the acceptance and support of their own families.

Soon, we too were in tears. In part, ours were tears of pleasure and gratitude for the stirring welcome. But they were also tears of sorrow for the personal anguish that obviously fueled this powerful response. They were tears of regret for millions of families throughout the country that had been senselessly torn apart and were in desperate need of help. It was a searing personal experience that would leave an indelible mark on each of us.

That night, as on the night Bobbi came out to us, I lay in bed reviewing a life-changing experience. I thought about how parents like myself, joined together in large enough numbers, could stem the tide of tragedy I had sensed that afternoon. And I pledged myself to the P-FLAG mission of fighting the deadly prejudice that threatened the well-being, and sometimes the very lives, of our gay kids.

Four months later I described my newfound commitment to P-FLAG in a *New York Times* column that was reprinted widely around the country. "My daughter is a lesbian," I wrote. "She also is the light of my life, a talented young woman whose joyous spirit helps brighten the lives of others." I wrote of the soul-shaking experience of the march on Washington. I told of my vision of a day when parents by the millions would enlist in the crusade for their gay kids' dignity. I pleaded the cause of "the most basic of freedoms: the right to be what one is."

The one-time admirer of a gay-basher had become a brazen booster of equality for homosexual citizens. But I still had a lot to learn about the history and makeup of the organization that had brought me to this point; about the legions of inspiring, courageous parents and young people I would be joining in a crusade against ignorance and apathy; about some darker sides of well-meaning social and religious traditions; and about the ominous forces of self-righteous, often self-serving, extremism that in the name of a loving God can tear families asunder.

4

◆

The Birth of a Movement

P-FLAG's pioneer mother is a slender, mild-mannered elementary school teacher named Jeanne Manford. In 1972, armed with a homemade sign, she touched off a parental revolution.

At that time, police were still raiding gay bars and arresting the patrons. Homosexuality was formally classified as a mental illness. Physical attacks on gays were a matter of total indifference to police. Gays were subject to arrest simply for being gay.

Jeanne cannot explain why, in such a hostile climate, she was not upset when she and her husband Jules learned their son Morty was gay. She wasn't so naive that she didn't recognize the stigma attached to being gay. But she loved Morty, and she told him that whatever made him happy was fine with her.

Jeanne was then in her fourth year at P.S. 32, a half-block away from the Flushing, New York house where she still lives. She would ultimately spend twenty-six peaceful years teaching the neighborhood youngsters. But her calm, competent schoolroom manner masked a fiercely protective parental instinct that surfaced in her personal life.

In the early 1970s, Morty was a student at Columbia University. He was also a pioneer gay rights activist, having founded one of the first gay campus organizations. (He later was an early president of one of the original gay rights groups, the Gay Activists Alliance.) So as perhaps was inevitable, Jeanne got a call from the police one night at 1 AM. Morty had been arrested. "And you know," the officer added ominously, "he's homosexual."

Jeanne was stung to anger. "I know that. Why are you bothering him? Why don't you go after criminals and stop harassing gays?"

Morty, standing near the police officer, didn't hear what his mother had said. But he saw the officer scratching his head in astonishment after he put down the phone.

The incident that would ultimately give rise to the family movement now known as P-FLAG occurred in early 1972. While handing out leaflets at a political gathering in New York City, Morty was attacked by the president of the New York City firemen's union, a former Golden Gloves champion. Police officers stood and watched as the man beat Morty and pushed him down a stairwell. Morty was hospitalized and had to take painkillers for a week.

Jeanne was furious. What right did they have to assault her son? Why didn't the police protect him? What kind of police force did New York have? Her lifelong restraint dissolved in anger. Nobody could walk over Morty like that.

She telephoned the New York Times, but they kept hanging up on her. So she fired off a letter to the New York Post expressing her outrage, particularly at the police for doing nothing. It was printed, and suddenly she was a celebrity of sorts. New Yorkers were amazed that a mother would speak out on behalf of her gay son. Among the most amazed were Morty's friends, who found it hard to believe his mother would actually say publicly, "I have a homosexual son, and I love him."

As a result of her letter, the entire family found itself in demand by television talk shows. Jeanne, Jules, and Morty appeared together in Boston and Cincinnati, and Jeanne and Jules did other shows in New Orleans, Detroit, and Toronto. These were the first of more than fifty television appearances that Jeanne would make, including on major shows such as *Donahue.*

The publicity drew waves of response from parents of gay children, and the Manfords began to sense the need for a parents' organization. The final impetus in that direction came in June 1972, when Morty asked his parents to march with him in the gay pride parade.

For Morty, the parade was a very special event, for he had been present at the incident that gave rise to the very concept of gay pride. This was the Stonewall Rebellion, and it represented a sort of gay Declaration of Independence. It occurred on June 28, 1969, when police raided the Stonewall Inn, a gay bar on Christopher Street in Greenwich Village. Unlike in earlier raids, the patrons decided they had had enough of police injustice. About two hundred of them resisted arrest, taunted the police, and threw bottles, rocks, and even their shoes at the officers. The next night, more demonstrations flared up, and the protests continued for five days. In other cities, rallies were held to support the New York uprising and to protest similar treatment of gays around the country. Stonewall became a symbol of rebellion and defiant self-respect that spread to gay communities throughout the nation.

Gay pride celebrations, held in commemoration of the Stonewall uprising, are now commonplace even in smaller cities. But to Morty—who had been in the Stonewall Inn when the police arrived—the second annual New York parade in 1972 still had immediate and intimate significance. Jeanne agreed to go with him, but only if Morty would help her make a sign she could carry. She had to let people know why she was marching. So they hand-lettered a cardboard sign: "Parents of Gays: Unite in Support for Our Children."

Jules couldn't attend the parade, and Jeanne carried the sign alone, walking next to Morty. The ovation was overwhelming. For the first few blocks, Jeanne assumed the wild cheering, shouting, and applause were for Dr. Benjamin Spock, the famed baby doctor, who was marching just behind her. But then young people began running up to *her*, crying, screaming, hugging her, kissing her, asking her if she would talk to their parents.

The idea of a parents' group took shape in her mind. As they marched, she and Morty discussed the possibility. At home, the Manfords' telephone rang constantly for days. It was clear that parents needed a place where they could talk to each other and know they were not alone. A place where they could hear others say there was nothing wrong with their kids.

Morty helped publicize the first meeting. He and a friend, writer Barbara Love, placed an ad in the *Village Voice*. They called other friends. They posted notices in bookstores and bars.

The first formal meeting was held in March 1973 in the Metropolitan Duane Methodist Church in Greenwich Village, by invitation of a sympathetic minister, Reverend Ed Egan. About twenty people—half of them parents, half of them young gays—were on hand for the historic occasion. Meetings were held monthly there for the next twenty years, until they were moved in 1992 to Community Church in midtown Manhattan.

The next major step in the movement came in the summer of 1974 when Jeanne and Jules, visiting in Los Angeles, met Adele and Larry Starr, who had a gay son. The two couples had dinner together, and the Manfords' exciting conversation about their experiences prompted Adele to try to start a Los Angeles group.

It was at first a frustrating task. "We called a meeting in 1975, but nobody came," Adele remembers ruefully. But she tried again in March 1976, and this time thirty-five people showed up. A West Coast counterpart of the Manfords' New York group was underway.

Meanwhile, other small support groups had been forming independently around the country. Betty Fairchild, the author of a still-popular 1976 book, *Now That You Know*, personally founded two groups, one in Washington, D.C., in 1974 and another in

Denver two years later. A St. Louis group was started by Marion and Art Wirth and Carolyn Griffin, authors of another popular book for parents, *Beyond Acceptance*. Others were beginning in cities such as Phoenix, Boston, Seattle, Anchorage, Pensacola, Baltimore, Kansas City (Missouri), Houston, and San Francisco. Gradually, members of the scattered groups found each other, often as the result of radio and television appearances by some of the more "out" parents, such as the Manfords and Starrs. A word-of-mouth network grew.

The first national meeting took place in Washington, D.C., in 1979, organized largely by Fairchild and a member of her group to coincide with that year's first-ever national march for gay rights. One highlight of the weekend was the appearance of two parents—Adele Starr and Dick Ashworth, a New York lawyer who had become a mainstay of the Manfords' group—addressing a major Mall rally.

As the crowds roared, Ashworth and Starr called for equal protection under the law for their gay children. Said Ashworth: "It is time for the world to realize that we parents of gays will support our children and fight for their rights." Said Starr: "They, and we, will not settle for less than their full rights in pursuit of happiness."

The following day, parents from around the country met in the First Congregational Church in Washington to talk about forming a national organization. It didn't happen right then, but a foundation was laid and the various groups kept in closer touch. Two years later, in the summer of 1981, P-FLAG was officially founded.

The organizing took place during a weekend meeting at the Starrs' Los Angeles home. Thirty-one representatives came from a variety of cities and towns—from New York City to Rifle, Colorado (population about 4,000). The location and timing arose from the fact that Dick and Amy Ashworth, who had two gay sons, were in California for the wedding of their third and only non-gay son.

In a marathon two-day session punctuated by frequent pizza

deliveries, the founders chose the organization's name and logo, adopted a statement of purpose, elected a board of directors, and assigned Dick Ashworth the task of incorporation. Adele Starr became P-FLAG's first president and Dick Ashworth the first chair of its board.

By the next summer, the organization was strong enough to hold its first national convention, in Los Angeles. It was both a proud and sad Jeanne Manford who attended. Her vision of a national organization of parents seeking justice for their gay children had come to pass. But that very first convention was dedicated to her husband, Jules, who had died earlier in 1982.

For the next several years, P-FLAG's national headquarters was Adele Starr's den, which served as an information clearinghouse and record storehouse. Slowly, new support groups started up throughout the country, in small towns as well as large cities. It wasn't always easy for the pioneering parents. In semi-rural Iowa, for example, a mother who had been president of her local church congregation was deposed and ostracized after forming a parents' group that, at first, met in her church. But in ten years the original handful of groups grew to nearly 250; and the larger chapter meetings, as in Denver, sometimes drew one hundred people or more. In 1989, a genuine national office was opened in Washington, D.C. And in 1990, Tom Sauerman of Philadelphia, a Lutheran pastor with a gay son, became the first executive director.

A decade of growth was celebrated at P-FLAG's tenth annual convention in Charlotte, North Carolina in 1991. There, "The Los Angeles 31" were honored by more than five hundred people at the Omni Charlotte Hotel. Among the emotion-choked speakers were Adele Starr and Amy Ashworth. Adele said the founders had been praised for their courage, but that courage was not involved: "We did it out of love and anger and a sense of injustice, and because we had to tell the world the truth about our children." Amy said she was embarrassed by the tribute, "because what we did is something that comes naturally—we love our children."

Once again, though, for Jeanne Manford, a milestone P-FLAG convention was an occasion of sadness. Morty was ill with AIDS, and she missed the meeting. Morty had once proclaimed, "The family that marches together, stays together," but death took him from the family in 1992.

"I will always love my son. I always thought he was extra special," Jeanne says. Nor did his death quell her dedication to combating anti-gay prejudice. The spunk that moved her to carry that sign in 1972 was apparent twenty years later, just weeks after Morty's death, when she faced down a notorious gay-baiter on a raucous *Geraldo* television show.

The show featured two young same-sex couples, each of whom had recently attended their high school proms. But attention was soon focused on two invited audience guests, Jeanne and a discredited psychologist named Paul Cameron.

Cameron has long been known in the media as an especially vicious apologist for homophobia. For many years, his condescending tone and tight-lipped smile of superiority were a frequent feature of sensationalist TV and radio talk shows. More recently, however, his appearances have dwindled since it became generally known that he was stripped of his membership in the American Psychological Association in 1983.

On *Geraldo*, Cameron seemed intent on needling Jeanne for having loved and supported her son. His persistent hostility ultimately enraged not only most of the studio audience but even Rivera himself. At one point, Cameron referred to Jeanne as a "poor woman" for having had a gay son. The remark brought her leaping to her feet, and she told Cameron heatedly, "I'm not a poor woman. . . . I can certainly hold my head up higher than anyone who has been thrown out of his professional association!" Her words were practically drowned in cheers.

In 1993, Jeanne organized yet another P-FLAG group, which met in her home until it grew too large and moved to a nearby church. In June of that year, as grand marshal of the first gay pride celebration held in her borough of Queens, New York, she basked in a five-minute ovation of gratitude from a cheering, whistling, stomping crowd.

Jeanne's courage and love were acclaimed in a column by Pulitzer Prize-winning writer Anna Quindlen, which was published in the *New York Times* shortly after Morty died. Quindlen described Jeanne as a mother who made history by standing by her son and who "wrote her unconditional love on poster paper for all the world to see." The column concluded:

> She loved and accepted her child the way he was. In a perfect world, this would be the definition of "parent" in the dictionary. The point is not what you'll tell your friends at the bridge table. It is what you'll tell yourself in the end.

Perhaps someday Jeanne Manford's accepting response will be typical of parents who learn they have a gay child. Perhaps a child's gayness will be no more unsettling than if he or she were left-handed. And perhaps no one will dream of defining a class of people by their sexual identity any more than by their eye color or taste in literature.

Don't hold your breath.

Pending that utopian day, gayness remains near the top of most Americans' lists of social stigmata. Thus, an organization like P-FLAG remains acutely needed. For too many parents, the point *is* indeed what they'll tell their friends at the bridge table.

Some become literally sick about what others might think. Harriet Dart, for example, became critically ill with asthma. Her doctor suggested she walk up to the first person she met after leaving his office and say, "Guess what? I have a gay son." He told her, "If they have an asthma attack, that's *their* problem. But if you have another one it will kill you."

So Harriet sought out the P-FLAG group in Rochester, New York, where she was then living. For a time, as for so many others, the organization became for her a sort of emergency first aid station. (Later, when she and her husband Bill moved to Detroit, they founded a P-FLAG chapter there, and Harriet became a tireless, articulate advocate and head of chapter development for the national organization.)

This type of rescue operation is one arm of P-FLAG's three-part mission: support, education, and advocacy. For "new" parents, the need for support is usually paramount. The peer group meetings—attended largely by parents with a sprinkling of young gays—often provide the first opportunity for traumatized parents to vent their often intense distress.

For most of life's crises, it's easy to find others who will support you. Death, illness, accident, and job loss are common occurrences for which others are quick to come to your side, to listen and understand and soothe. When you're hurting, you don't want to have to convince others of your pain—you want instant empathy. But after learning you have a gay child, it may seem that there is nowhere you can turn for solace. So a P-FLAG support meeting often provides the first safe haven for the relief of pent-up emotions. There, you can find that instant empathy. You don't have to pretend you're not feeling anger, grief, shame, guilt.

"It's just an incredible experience when you finally realize you're not alone," says Cathy Tuerk of Washington, D.C. "There's a kind of unconditional acceptance. You see others who have survived and are at different stages of the process of acceptance. It's encouraging to hear them remember how *they* felt when they first knew."

Those who have "survived" become role models. "We get to help others," says a father. "It gives us a sense of our own progress and strength. It's really empowering."

Education, the second arm of P-FLAG's mission, is an important aspect of the support process itself. Parents and other kin ultimately move to acceptance, and beyond, largely because of what they learn—and unlearn—about homosexuality.

P-FLAG's education function reaches far beyond the support groups and into the mainstream. To this end, it utilizes publications, fact sheets, reading lists, cassettes, conferences, seminars, and speaker bureaus. The most effective teaching agents, however, are P-FLAG members themselves. Newly educated, legions of parents are moved to pass on what they've learned to their schools, churches, community organizations, and government officials. And national P-FLAG is now planning an historic multimedia public education program known as Project Open Mind. Designed to alter public images of gay people, it is expected to become the largest such campaign ever undertaken.

Advocacy, the final facet of P-FLAG's mission, clearly overlaps with education. In a sense, advocacy is simply education applied to points of political leverage—voting blocs or public bodies—to attain particular ends such as equal rights measures or broader sex education. For P-FLAGgers are convinced that when Americans learn the truth about homosexuality, their sense of fairness will not allow them to continue to discriminate against our gay kids.

When that happens, P-FLAG's mission will have been fulfilled. Education and advocacy will have generated the ultimate instrument of family support: a society in which parents will have no reason to lament having a gay child. It will be a society in which Jeanne Manford's nonchalance about her son's coming out will be the parental norm.

And P-FLAG will no longer have any reason to exist.

5

♦

Families Fighting the Myths

I t's no mystery why families are devastated by the disclosure that they have a gay member. Most Americans simply assume that homosexuals are sinful, sick, or both. The assumption is not only untrue, it is classic irony.

Scores of history's most creative, influential, and inspiring humans have been gay. A short list includes the philosophers Socrates and Plato; famed rulers such as Alexander the Great, Hadrian, King Richard I (the Lion-Hearted), and Peter the Great; artists Leonardo da Vinci and Michelangelo; poets such as Lord Byron and Walt Whitman; writers Sir Francis Bacon, Hans Christian Andersen, Henry Thoreau, Herman Melville, D. H. Lawrence, Henry James, Willa Cather, Gertrude Stein, Virginia Woolf, Marcel Proust, Vita Sackville-West, Somerset Maugham, James Baldwin, E. M. Forster, and Andre Gide; playwrights Oscar Wilde and Tennessee Williams; composers Peter Tchaikovsky, Cole Porter, and Aaron Copland; dancer Rudolph Nureyev; military leader T. E. Lawrence; and economist John Maynard Keynes. And this list, of course, includes only some of those we know about. Legions of past greats shall ever remain closeted.

Today, throughout society, a few leaders in various fields are beginning to come out. In sports these include tennis greats

Martina Navratilova and Billie Jean King, Olympic gold medal diver Greg Louganis, and NFL veteran Dave Kopay. In entertainment there are Ian McKellen, Dick Sargent, Elton John, k. d. lang, and Harvey Fierstein. In religion there is Episcopal Bishop Otis Charles. In journalism, *New Republic* editor Andrew Sullivan and syndicated columnist Deb Price. In literature, Edward Albee, Tony Kushner, Gore Vidal, Rita Mae Brown, Paul Monette, and Armistead Maupin. And in Congress, one Republican, Steve Gunderson of Wisconsin, and two Democrats, Barney Frank and Gerry Studds of Massachusetts.

Any such lists are, admittedly, seriously incomplete. But they make an important commentary on common stereotypes.

I have met hundreds of lesbians and gay men whose lives would make any parent proud. Some are professionals—competent and respected physicians, lawyers, architects, professors, artists, authors, and so on. Others are memorable because of highly attractive personal characteristics: compassion, humor, imagination, talent. Many are in long-term, life-enhancing relationships, and most are living productive and rewarding lives. They evoke affection and respect. My life is richer for knowing them.

To be sure, the gay community has its share of psychological misfits. But the notion that being gay in itself means being sick or sinful is a groundless myth.

The medical profession for years dealt with homosexuality as a personality disorder. The notion was fueled by early studies that looked only at gay men who had sought psychological counseling. The logic therefore was based on a glaring non sequitur—since gay patients who sought psychiatric help were maladjusted, *all* gays must be maladjusted.

Psychiatric myths about homosexuals, particularly gay men, are nevertheless still given credence by many nonprofessionals. Perhaps the most widespread misconception is that gayness stems from an unhealthy home environment—the most popular villains being a dominant, smothering mother and a passive or indifferent father. Until recently, many psychiatrists talked seriously about a "homosexual personality" that classified gays as vindictive and aggressive, unable to sustain healthy relationships. All such theories have been thoroughly discredited.

Dr. Evelyn Hooker, a research psychologist, was the first to point out the anomaly of judging all homosexuals by samples limited to those under psychological treatment. A heterosexual with numerous gay friends, Hooker was struck by the discrepancy between prevailing medical views and her friends' robust mental health. So she undertook her own government-funded study in 1957, applying intensive personality testing to a random group of gays and a matched group of non-gays. The study's case files, including all the standard diagnostic psychological profiles, were analyzed by a panel of psychiatrists, who had of course been trained to believe that to be gay was to be mentally ill. Nonetheless, they were unable to distinguish gays from non-gays. The results stunned the psychological world.

Sixteen years later, in 1973, the American Psychiatric Association (APA) finally got around to removing homosexuality from its list of disorders. In doing so, the APA stated that there was no reason why a lesbian or gay man couldn't be just as healthy, effective, law-abiding, and productive as any heterosexual. The American Psychological Association and the American Bar Association soon adopted similar standards.

It is appropriate that Hooker is now an honorary director of P-FLAG, for her studies pointed out what P-FLAG parents almost invariably come to realize—that the notion of homosexuality as illness is simply a reflection of social norms. Hooker compares it to what was once said to be a psychological maladjustment among slaves. Their symptom was running away from the plantation.

No less irrational—but perhaps even more profoundly ingrained in the social consciousness—is the widespread view that homosexuality is sinful. Most major American religious groups still formally hew to that line. Only a few—notably the United Church of Christ, Unitarian-Universalism, and Reform Judaism—ordain openly gay ministers or rabbis, and only a tiny minority of American clergy will conduct same-sex ceremonies of union. (By contrast, gay marriage is now legal in Norway, Denmark, and Sweden.)

Normally, the Bible is cited as the ultimate justification for unequivocal condemnation of homosexuality. In fact, however, the Good Book is ambiguous on the subject. Consider, for example, the famous story of Sodom and Gomorrah, from which the word *sodomy* comes and which undergirds the radical right's angry denunciation of gays as "sodomites." In the view of most serious Biblical scholars, the actual targets of the passage are inhospitality and indifference to the poor. Peter J. Gomes, Professor of Christian Morals at Harvard, wrote in 1992, "To suggest that Sodom and Gomorrah is about homosexual sex is an analysis of about as much worth as suggesting that the story of Jonah and the whale is a treatise on fishing."

The most explicit Biblical condemnation of homosexuality is in Leviticus, where it is labeled an "abomination." But the same book also proscribes such matters as wearing garments with two different kinds of yarn, planting two different kinds of seed in the same field, eating raw meat, and touching the skin of a dead pig. So to be consistent, people who quote Leviticus to condemn homosexuality should among other things avoid playing football, particularly while wearing a polyester-cotton blend warm-up suit.

As for the New Testament, there is no indication that Jesus ever mentioned homosexuals or homosexuality. He simply related a message of love, charity, and acceptance of all of God's creatures. Passages seemingly negative to homosexuality derive from Paul, but many Biblical scholars see these primarily as proscriptions against what might be called "unnaturalness." While it is natural for a heterosexual to make love to someone of the opposite gender, the same act is quite unnatural for a lesbian or gay man. And can there in any event be anything more natural, whatever the gender of the partners, than a sincere love that contributes to a couple's growth and fullness-of-being?

Despite this shaky Biblical basis, homosexuality has long been assumed to be a sin, an unquestioned evil in the same way as murder, rape, and incest were. Only now—and only with severe attendant social upheaval—is the notion giving way. We are learning that same-sex attraction, while a minority trait, is no less natural than heterosexuality.

Recent research strongly suggests that sexual orientation might have a significant genetic component, and in any event is strongly influenced by biochemical events prior to birth. In 1993, Dr. Dean Hamer of the National Institutes of Health discovered a likely genetic link to homosexuality in the X chromosome; among forty pairs of homosexual brothers, he found that thirty-three had inherited the same set of five genetic markers on their X chromosomes. Two years earlier, a Salk Institute neuroscientist, Dr. Simon LeVay, found striking differences in the brain anatomy of gay and non-gay men. In 1994, two Canadian researchers even found a statistically significant difference in fingerprint patterns, which develop in the fetus, between groups of gay and heterosexual males. Research teams from Northwestern University, Boston University, and Johns Hopkins University have all found strong evidence of genetic factors in homosexuality; and they agree that sexual orientation is in any event fixed by the first few years of life.

There is no respectable scientific data to suggest that once set, sexual orientation is amenable to change. Sexual *behavior* can be altered, just as a left-handed person can be forced to write with his or her right hand. But in either instance, the person will be acting against his or her true nature.

The late Sylvia Pennington was a Pentecostal minister who set out to "save" gays by prayer and persuasion. But she ultimately concluded that they were instead damaged, maimed, scarred, and even killed by the well-meaning ex-gay ministries that purport to "cure" homosexuality. When one religious-oriented book was written about six gays who were supposedly "changed" to heterosexuals, Pennington noted, all six subjects soon provided the book's publisher with notarized statements that they had remained homosexual.

Dr. Keith Brodie, a former president of the American Psychiatric Association and later president of Duke University, agrees with Pennington. Mental health therapy to change sexual orientation, he says, "is about as successful as the handedness change, and about as painful, and also about as ludicrous."

And in 1994, no less than the American Medical Association formally rejected the concept of "reparative" therapy designed to change sexual orientation. The organization finally acknowledged the obvious—that if gays experience emotional disturbance associated with their orientation, it probably stems from "a sense of alienation in an unaccepting environment." In other words, anti-gay social attitudes are bad for mental health.

Michael Bussee was a co-founder of Exodus International, one of the ministries to which Pennington referred. After five years with the group, he says he realized that the program not only had never changed a single person, but was actually doing a lot of harm. A forty-five-year-old Californian, Jack McIntyre, killed himself a year after signing up with an ex-gay ministry; he wrote in his suicide note that "no matter how much I prayed and tried to avoid temptation, I continually failed." Another disillusioned subject of such a ministry told a press conference that frustration had led him to mutilate his own genitals.

The central irony in these tragedies was captured by an observation made by a young lesbian I met shortly after she spent a year in one of the ex-gay programs in the Midwest. When we spoke, she was living with a Maryland P-FLAG couple, recovering from the emotional scars left by the program. A formerly devout Catholic, she said she had thought about suicide while in the program—but that the worst part of the experience was that it threatened to destroy her own sense of spirituality. These so-called ministries, in short, tend to kill the very quality they purport to save.

Perhaps the strongest clerical voice for equality for lesbians and gay men is that of Episcopal Bishop John Shelby Spong. "It is clear," Spong has written, "that heterosexual prejudice against homosexuals must take its place alongside witchcraft, slavery, and other ignorant beliefs and oppressive institutions that we have abandoned." But enlightenment comes slowly. Most of us are taught as youngsters that homosexuality is a heinous evil. And despite any subsequent overlays of intellectual sophistication, such early conditioning permanently shapes our perceptions. So it is hardly surprising that parents often make serious mistakes in dealing with their gay kids, and P-FLAG ranks are filled with those who regret their initial responses.

The stories of five such families make the point: Mary Griffith told her son he needed to pray harder to overcome his homosexual feelings. Cathy and Jonathan Tuerk subjected their eight-year-old son to psychotherapy to make him "more masculine." Marie Pridgen convinced her son to enter an ex-gay ministry to change his orientation. Sue Brown took her daughter to two psychiatrists to be "cured." Betty and Jim Holloran were estranged from their physician son for six years because they viewed him as a willful sinner.

Two of the children in these examples are dead. All of them suffered because of their parents' well-meaning mistakes. Ultimately, the parents all concluded that it was they and not their children whose behavior needed to change.

Mary Griffith's story is a P-FLAG legend. For Mary, it reflects the ultimate human tragedy, for she blames herself for the death of her son Bobby.

Mary says Bobby was "kind and gentle, with a fun-loving spirit." He was handsome, with clean-cut features and an Adonis-like body perfected by weightlifting. He loved old movies, particularly *The Seven Year Itch* with his favorite star, Marilyn Monroe. He loved Italian food and meeting people.

But the diary that he kept for the last two years of his life reveals a tortured soul. Tortured by passions he had been taught were sinful. Tortured by the bondage of what he called "society's rules." Tortured by fear of Hell. "Gays are bad," he wrote, "and God sends bad people to Hell. . . . I guess I'm no good to anyone, not even God. Sometimes I feel like disappearing from the face of this earth."

The Griffiths attended Walnut Creek Presbyterian Church in Walnut Creek, California. There, Mary said, the ministers and the congregation were clear that homosexuals were sick, perverted, and condemned to eternal damnation. "And when they said that," Mary recalls, "I said, 'Amen.'"

For her part, Mary just knew that homosexuality was "an abomination to God." And even before she knew Bobby was gay, she conveyed her feelings to him in no uncertain terms. She remembers in sadness one incident that occurred when Bobby was fourteen. He had introduced her to a friend of his, a young girl. For some reason, Mary had loaned the girl a coat. Later, Mary learned that the girl had once had a lesbian encounter, and found herself unable to wear the coat again herself. "You can't love God and be gay," she told Bobby.

At about the same time, Bobby told his brother he was gay. Two years later, his brother told their parents. That night, the family was up until 4 AM talking and crying. They all agreed Bobby was a sinner, that he had to be cured by prayer and Christian counseling. Mary told him he had to repent or God would "damn him to hell and eternal punishment." She had faith that God would come to Bobby's rescue, but only if he read his Bible.

The Christian counselor recommended prayer and suggested that Bobby spend more time with his father. But Bobby's diary revealed that nothing was changing. "Why did you do this to me,

God?" he wrote. "Am I going to hell? . . . I need your seal of approval. If I had that, I would be happy. Life is so cruel and unfair."

His mother kept telling him he could change. "It seems like every time we talked, I would tell him that," she says. "I thought Bobby wasn't trying in his prayers." When Bobby became more withdrawn, she simply chalked it up to God's punishment. "Now," she says, "I look back and realize he was just depressed."

When Bobby was twenty, in desperation the Griffiths decided he should move to Portland, Oregon and live with a cousin. At first, the move seemed to help. He worked as a nurse's aid in a senior citizens' home and developed something of a social life. But the depression returned and deepened. A few months later, in his diary, he cursed God and added, "I'm completely worthless as far as I'm concerned. What do you say to that? I don't care." Again and again, he emphasized the shame and self-blame he felt over his sexual orientation. "I am evil and wicked. I am dirt," he wrote. "My voice is small and unheard, unnoticed, damned."

One Friday night in August 1983, Bobby had dinner with his cousin. She noticed that he seemed thoughtful, perhaps depressed. He seemed to want to talk about something, but said little. Then he left, saying he was taking a bus to go dancing downtown.

Early the next morning, two men driving to work noticed a young man, later identified as Bobby, on an overpass above a busy thoroughfare. As they described the next few moments, the boy walked to the railing, turned around, and did a sudden backflip into mid-air. He landed in the path of an eighteen-wheeler.

Bobby's body was returned to Walnut Creek for funeral services in the Presbyterian church. The minister told the mourners that Bobby was gay, and suggested that his tragic end was the result of his sinning.

Later, the Griffiths met with their pastor for grief counseling. In her despair, Mary was seeking ways to atone for the loss of Bobby. She told the pastor she knew there were "other Bobbys out there" and asked how she could help them. The pastor merely shrugged his shoulders—and Mary never again returned to that church.

However, she did not lose her sense of religion. Her speech resonates with the tones of spiritual awareness. But she has found a very different God from the one she worshipped at Walnut Creek Presbyterian. She reread her Bible with fresh eyes, and sought out secular books about homosexuality. She concluded that there was nothing wrong with Bobby, that "he was the kind of person God wanted him to be . . . an equal, lovable, valuable part of God's creation." She says now, "I helped instill false guilt in an innocent child's conscience."

Bobby Griffith's fate is not uncommon among gay youth. One report chartered by the government suggests that gay adolescents are nearly three times more likely than other teens to attempt suicide. Some 30 percent of *all* youth suicides, it says, can be traced to the pressures generated by "a society that stigmatizes and discriminates against gays and lesbians."

But Bobby's story stands out for two reasons. Unlike other youths who kill themselves, Bobby left an extensive written record of his anguish. And unlike other parents, his mother has not denied or buried her role in the tragedy, but has leveraged her remorse into aid to others.

Shortly after Bobby's death, Mary Griffith discovered P-FLAG. For some years, she has been president of an East San Francisco Bay P-FLAG chapter. She appears frequently on television talk shows, usually wearing a button with Bobby's picture and another with the P-FLAG message, "We love our gay and lesbian children." She has cooperated in the filming of documentaries about the Griffith family tragedy, and is the subject of the book *Prayers for Bobby: A Mother's Coming to Terms with the Suicide of Her Gay Son* by Leroy Aarons, founder of the National Lesbian and Gay Journalists Association and a former national correspondent for the *Washington Post*. She campaigns tirelessly for the cause of public school counseling supportive of gay teenagers, believing that

Bobby would still be alive if his high school had had such a program.

And she has a guiding standard for other parents. Listen to your instincts as a mother or father, she tells them, not to those who urge you to violate your parental conscience. "All we had to do was say, 'We love you, Bobby, and we accept you,' and I know Bobby would be here today. Part of me wanted to reach out and tell him, 'You're fine just the way you are.' To me, that was my mother love, that was my conscience. But I didn't have the freedom to listen to my own conscience."

Like Mary Griffith, Catherine and Jonathan Tuerk were betrayed by the institution they respected above all others. For Griffith, it was her church. For the Tuerks, it was their profession.

Catherine and Jonathan are both pyschotherapists: she a nurse practitioner with a private clientele, he a psychiatrist at a world-famous hospital in Maryland. So when their little boy Joshua acted in what to them seemed inappropriate ways, they sent him to a psychiatrist—as often as four times a week, off and on, for nearly a decade. Ultimately, they spent tens of thousands of dollars in an endeavor that they now feel merely deepened Josh's insecurity and their own guilt.

The problem, as they saw it, was that Josh from infancy was more interested in "girl things" than in "boy things." In nursery school, he played with the girls in the dress-up room. On the playground, he shied away from the rough-housing of the other boys. When they gave him toy cars, instead of making them go "VROOM! VROOM!" he would play relationship games, calling one the "mommy car," another the "daddy car." When he played with the neighborhood children, he usually teamed with Tina, the girl next door, against the other boys. He spent a lot of time with Tina, because his interests seemed to mesh more with hers than with those of the other boys.

When Josh was six, his parents consulted a well-known child

psychiatrist. In retrospect, the prescription they were given might as well have come from an anthology of old wives' tales: Josh should play contact sports and do more things with his father.

So they tried him at football, lacrosse, baseball, and basketball. Jonathan even took a turn at coaching Josh's soccer team. But nothing worked. Josh tried hard to carry out his parents' wishes, but he remained frightened and miserable. His only partial success came in karate, which in general he hated: he won a prize for form.

Meanwhile, when he was eight, his parents started sending him to psychotherapy to build his self-esteem and thereby, they hoped, help him grow up more masculine. Although he usually came home from these sessions looking sad, his parents were convinced that the short-term pain would produce long-term gain. Ultimately, Cathy thought, "he wouldn't be gay, and then he could be happy."

But at age nine, Josh wrote in his diary, "I hate myself. I think I'm a fag." And twelve years later, he told his parents the words they had for so long been dreading: he was gay. (When one of his former neighborhood playmates learned of that, his surprised response was, "How can that be? He always had that thing going with Tina.")

The Tuerks finally decided they had been tilting at windmills. Ultimately, Jonathan resigned from the American Psychoanalytic Association—dissatisfied, among other things, with the analytic profession's slowness to acknowledge the degree to which sexual orientation might be innate and unchangeable.

Cathy is now president of the Washington, D.C. Metropolitan Area P-FLAG chapter. Her experience has led her to develop a special interest in educating parents about what she calls "gentle" boys—those who shun more macho pursuits in favor of the intellectual or artistic. A substantial number of such youngsters turn out to be heterosexual, just as a number of competitive, athletic types turn out to be gay. Cathy tries to show parents that they can

accept their children for whatever they are. (Recent studies have
led to increasing recognition of a so-called "sissy boy" syndrome
that *does* appear to be a relatively reliable indicator of homosexuality. Boys fitting the syndrome often, for example, enjoy playing
with dolls; and their behavior even at age four and five can be
quite effeminate. Usually, such behavior tends to become far less
noticeable after age eight, probably reflecting a surrender to social
norms.)

To Cathy, the implications for parents are clear. Fighting the
inevitable is more than a waste of time. It can boomerang in cruel
fashion. As she now sees it: "At the age of twenty-one, Josh decided to be himself. My son was born gay. I know it."

Marie Pridgen of Wilmington, North Carolina, says that when her
son Crae told her he was gay, "I was a crazy parent stuck up there
on the ceiling for a while. . . . I even went to the bars, and pulled
him out and preached to his friends in the bars. I did things a
crazy parent does."

At one point, when he was considering marrying a girlfriend,
Crae consulted his minister about his attraction to men. The minister and he prayed together. When they were done, the minister
told Crae, "Go home. You're healed." Of course, his feelings
remained unchanged, and Crae wisely refrained from marrying.

Marie prevailed upon Crae to enroll in an ex-gay ministry in
California in an effort to change his orientation. But after about
six months, they both decided the venture was not only worthless but potentially harmful.

Marie is devoutly religious, and attends a Presbyterian church
in Wilmington. She turned to the church for help, and there, fortunately, found relief from her anguish. For one thing, her minister was sympathetic to gay concerns; he even delivered a sermon
on homosexuality, explaining that gays, like everyone else, are simply looking for love and acceptance.

The church also housed a support group for parents of gay

children. It stressed the importance of unconditional love to their children, and helped Marie change her ways. "I thought, 'Hey, that's my child and I love him.' I hadn't been helping him. I was just destroying a relationship."

Marie's fifteen minutes of fame came in early 1993 during the gays-in-the-military flap, when Crae, then twenty-nine, was beaten and severely injured by three Marines in Wilmington. According to news reports, as the Marines were pummeling Crae they shouted, "Clinton must pay, all you faggots are going to die." A police officer told the *New York Times* that the Marines later showed no remorse and said they hated all homosexuals and were "not ashamed of it."

The incident became the focus of high-level meetings in the White House and Pentagon; and Crae and Marie were flown to Washington to sit in. On Capitol Hill, they visited the offices of several senators who expressed outrage over the incident. In a Capitol corridor, they were recognized by Hillary Clinton, who approached them to express her own sympathies.

In the next few days, Marie and Crae made a series of media appearances together, including *The Today Show*, *Dateline*, and *Faith Daniels* and *Sally Jesse Raphael*. The *Dateline* broadcast ended with a close-up of Marie, tense with emotion, responding to a question on whether the events had made her afraid: "I'm not only afraid for my own life and my son's life," she said, "but for every American who stands up for what's right."

In 1979, Sue Brown chanced to overhear a romantic conversation between her fifteen-year-old daughter Cody and another girl. Sue confronted Cody, who confirmed that she was gay. Groping for consolation, Sue compared homosexuality to the dangers of drug addiction. "At least this isn't going to kill you," she said to Cody. Her daughter replied, "Mother, I've already tried to kill myself."

So Sue took her to a psychiatrist. "She said there was nothing wrong with my daughter, that I had homophobia," Sue recalls.

They consulted a second psychotherapist, who said essentially the same thing.

Mother and daughter conspired to keep the news from Cody's father; meanwhile, Sue found P-FLAG and attended meetings regularly. After a few years of this secrecy, Sue one day called Cody, who was by then in college: it was time to come out to her father. Sue was planning to march with P-FLAG in the gay pride parade that weekend, and it was possible her husband might see her. Cody rushed home to break the news to her father, but he was not as accepting as Sue. Their differing reactions to Cody's gayness became one of the issues that led to their divorce in 1991.

In 1992, Sue was interviewed by Barbara Bartucci for a *Woman's Day* article about P-FLAG. During one telephone call, Bartucci heard what she called "tinkly party sounds" on Sue's end. Sue explained that she was holding a reception following a Methodist ceremony of union for Cody and Julie Marria. At one point, Sue excused herself to talk with someone. When she returned to the call, she said that the voice in the background was that of "my daughter-in-law Julie."

In her article, Bartucci wrote: "Her daughter-in-law, I thought. She means her daughter's female partner. The naturalness of the phrase—the loving acceptance those words implied—touched me." The author described the incident as one that "defines a healthy relationship between a parent and a homosexual child."

By the time of that party, Sue had long been a P-FLAG activist. Among other things, she continues to open her house to gay teenagers whose parents have ejected them from their own homes; they stay with Sue until their parents, in her words, "become educated," or until the youngsters finish high school and can live on their own.

The *Washington Post Magazine* cover story for December 7, 1986, was "The Bittersweet Life of Jimmy Holloran." It began this way:

He had it all—looks, brains, startling athletic ability. Then he had a falling out with his parents and his church over his homosexuality, and left for a new life in San Francisco. After he got AIDS 14 years later, he did the only thing a beloved son could do. He came home to die.

Jimmy was an honor student and president of the student council in his Washington, D.C. high school, and is in the school's athletic hall of fame as a running back on the school's city championship team. He won a national high school poetry contest, and thought he might become a priest. He turned down a scholarship to Harvard in order to attend Holy Cross, a Catholic college.

At Holy Cross, he was all-New England on a baseball team that twice played in the College World Series. As a senior, he scored higher than anyone before him on the Harvard medical school entrance exam. After graduating from medical school and serving his internship, he became head of an emergency room at a hospital in San Francisco. There, he also produced film documentaries, including an award-winning medical film about AIDS.

One evening, Jimmy telephoned his parents, Jim and Betty, from San Francisco to tell them he was gay. He asked them to accept him as a gay man. But no matter how much they loved him, they just couldn't do that. They were ashamed of him. Their Catholicism told them he was a sinner. To Jim and Betty, Jimmy had tossed away his faith and was acting reprehensibly. Every time they went to church, they prayed for his salvation. Jimmy was offended by their attitude, and virtually stopped talking to them.

Six unhappy years passed in this fashion; then Jimmy learned he had AIDS. He didn't tell his parents until he was seriously ill and hospitalized in San Francisco. In the face of this crisis, questions of faith faded in importance, and Jim and Betty went to San Francisco. Their attitude toward homosexuality began to thaw in the aura of warmth and caring they found emanating from his friends there. When they returned to Washington, they sought out help and found P-FLAG. Increasingly, they found themselves questioning the plausibility of their church's stance on homosexuality, and in Jimmy's final illness, they attained a more meaningful closeness with him. Jimmy spent his last months in the family home, surrounded by his parents, his three brothers, and his sister. Jim and Betty regretted the years they had missed being with him because they hadn't accepted him as he was. But they now offered prayers of thanks for the time they still had together.

In the face of harsh religious objections from relatives and friends, Betty became a champion of Catholics with AIDS and their families. After Jimmy died in 1986, she volunteered at an AIDS hospice and collected clothing and furniture for those living there. She worked with the families of people with AIDS, and conducted workshops on coming out to parents, for people with HIV and AIDS, at both a national P-FLAG convention and an International Gay and Lesbian Health Conference.

During virtually the entire time of her service to families touched by AIDS, Betty herself was terminally ill. In December 1991, she died of cancer.

Perhaps the most courageous thing she and Jim did was going public with the family's tale via that *Washington Post Magazine* cover story. It triggered animosity within their church and among their own relatives. But it also brought warm responses of gratitude, evidenced by a thick file of thank-you letters and accolades from priests and parishioners.

Veronica and Jerry Colfer (see Chapter 3) are among the Catholics inspired by Betty Holloran's work. Now vocal and articulate critics of their church's anti-gay stance, the Colfers have attracted considerable media attention. Betty would probably endorse one of Veronica's oft-quoted observations: "Families were here before churches."

6

◆

The Radical Challenge
One Family Under Siege

The parents discussed in Chapter 5 became activists after realizing that common misconceptions about homosexuality had savaged their families. For most of them, as is often the case, the process leading up to this realization took several years. But now, many parents are finding that they don't have the luxury of such a leisurely schooling.

The reason is a significant new threat: a concerted nationwide campaign to crystallize homophobic prejudice into law. In practice, this takes the form of anti-gay ballot initiatives backed by powerful, organized, well-financed groups of the so-called "religious right." The mildest initiatives are aimed at prohibiting public bodies from acting to prevent discrimination based on sexual orientation. But some initiatives go much further—even to proscribing the mere mention of homosexuality in other than condemning terms. Prototypes of such initiatives were first tested in 1992 in Oregon and Colorado.

The campaigns waged around these initiatives prodded a number of families out of the relative comfort of the closet and into unaccustomed activism. This and the next chapter examine the stories of some of these familes.

*   *   *

If approved, Oregon's Ballot Measure 9 would have enshrined gay-hatred in the state constitution. It would have prohibited any state agency from any act that might "promote, condone, encourage, or facilitate" homosexual behavior. Its scope was sufficiently broad to reach anyone remotely involved with state agencies who might mention homosexuality in less than pejorative terms.

In Ashland, P-FLAG Northwest Regional Director Candace Steele worried that her state counseling license might be in jeopardy. In Portland, chapter President Kathryn Warrior had similar concerns about her teaching credentials. They were among a handful of parents who took early stands against Number 9. But the numbers of open opponents would grow as the mean-spirited tone of the Pro-9 campaign jarred parents out of their silence.

Some of us, because of where we live and what we do for a living, risk little by openly supporting our gay children. But a lot of parents aren't so lucky. Many fear, often rightly, that too much candor could jeopardize their jobs or the jobs of their gay children. Many belong to churches that denounce homosexuality as sinful. And many live in small communities that seem poised to punish the slightest deviation from bedrock conformity.

Jim and Elise Self lived quietly in that kind of place—Grants Pass, Oregon, a small lumber and farming town of about 18,000 souls—until the radical right converted them into reluctant activists. They didn't win over their town, but they did discover a lot of new friends.

Jim, a physician, and Elise, a preschool teacher, had been high school sweethearts in Raleigh, North Carolina. Although their conservative Southern upbringing helped them fit in to the small-town life when they moved to Grants Pass in 1977, the Selfs were initially attracted to the area in part because of the easygoing cultural climate that prevailed then. As the seat of Josephine County, located in the Rogue River Valley, one of the country's premier white water locales, the town had long been a recreation mecca for rafters, canoers, and kayakers. The area was then also known as "Easy Valley" because of its perceived live-and-let-live attitude. Hippie communes were common there in the 1960s and 1970s, and as Jim says, "It was just a place where everybody came and did their own thing."

During the 1980s, however, moral rigidity set in. By 1991, Josephine County counted more than fifty conservative churches devoted to a staunchly patriarchal tradition.

Despite the changing atmosphere, the Selfs flourished in Grants Pass. They raised two gifted and popular children, Robert and Jennifer. Their lives centered on their careers, their friends, and the education and extracurricular activities of their children. Jim and Elise were prime movers in the PTA and in the Boosters Club. Jim served as volunteer physician for the high school football team, and Elise was a director of the five-county Winema Council of the Girl Scouts of America. The family often spent weekends and vacations camping and canoeing through the mountains and beaches of the Pacific Northwest.

In short, the Selfs were pillars of conventionality in a locale where supporting gay rights could in the best of times threaten careers and friendships and evoke social ostracism. And 1991— when the Selfs learned their daughter Jennifer was gay—was not the best of times in Oregon. It was the year in which an ugly cloud of bigotry and violence was descending over the state. And the cloud was darkest in rural areas such as Grants Pass.

An important influence in the rightward shift in Grants Pass was the founding in the 1980s of the Oregon Citizens Alliance (OCA), a religion-oriented spin-off of the Oregon Republican Party. The OCA scored its first major triumph in 1988, when it sponsored an initiative that overturned an executive order banning discrimination in state hiring based on sexual orientation. In 1991, the organization found its full homophobic voice when it launched a petition drive promoting what would become Ballot Measure 9.

The OCA collected the necessary signatures, and its measure

was placed on the 1992 general ballot. Number 9 did not simply call for the repeal of existing gay rights ordinances in three cities and the banning of their adoption elsewhere in the state; it equated gayness with pedophilia, sadism, and masochism. If passed, it would establish as a constitutional tenet—and as required teaching in all the state's public schools and colleges—that homosexuality is "abnormal, wrong, unnatural, and perverse." Besides the personal threat to his family, Jim worried with other physicans that the University of Oregon School of Medicine could lose its accreditation because of its failure to teach that homosexuality was perverse.

Jennifer's disclosure led Jim and Elise to join a hardy band of vastly outnumbered P-FLAG families who actively opposed Number 9 in the rural areas of Oregon. They spoke at community meetings, appeared on radio and television talk shows, handed out literature, and registered voters. They also put up with personal abuse. In nearby Ashland, a telephone caller told P-FLAGger Chuck Steele, "Wouldn't it be nice if all homosexuals were dead?" Another phoned the Steeles' friend and fellow P-FLAGger, Gerry Garland, to say, "You ought to be ashamed to have a fucking queer son." Moments after Garland hung up, the same man called back. "I forgot," he said. "Does the bastard have AIDS yet?"

The worst tragedy occurred in Salem, where a lesbian and a gay man were burned to death in an arson incident apparently triggered by campaign emotions. In Portland, the "No on 9" offices were burglarized and vandalized, and mailing lists were destroyed.

In Portland, Police Chief Tom Potter minimized the mayhem by assigning special units to prevent violence from either side. Potter was already a pet whipping-boy of the radical right because he supported his lesbian daughter, who was an officer on his force, and because he recruited other gay and lesbian officers. His efforts to calm the situation prompted death threats and calls for his resignation.

The Selfs, after receiving a number of angry letters, for the first time kept a loaded gun in the house. "I was that scared," Jim says. At times, he said, it seemed as though "an atmosphere of total fear" had descended on the gay community and its supporters. So it was that in little Grants Pass, amid the spectacular beauty of the Rogue River Valley, the Self family found themselves caught in the eye of a hurricane of hate. And so it is that their story differs so strikingly from that of those of us who risk little or nothing by supporting our gay children. Theirs is truly a story of high courage. It is a tale of genuine family values—a blend of personal integrity, compassion, pride, and faith in one another—that withstood the gales of hostility and ignorance loosed by moral fervor gone wild.

Jennifer Self was one of North Valley High's all-time outstanding scholar-athletes. While racking up the grades that made her class valedictorian, she was an all-state performer in basketball, volley-ball, and softball. She was a two-time participant in a prestigious local scholastic competition known as the Academic Masters con-test, and she won its top honors in English. She won a free-ride basketball scholarship to the University of California at Berkeley. There, while earning admission to a national honor society for psychology majors, she twice broke the school's season record for three-point shots. She is well known and, at least until 1992, high-ly regarded throughout Grants Pass and Josephine County. To her family, as Elise says, "she is warm and caring and sensitive and vulnerable and angry and sad, funny and human."

Of herself, however, Jennifer has written, "All those years I was growing up in Grants Pass and passing as the straight-laced-goody-two-shoes-heterosexual-egghead-jock, I was living in sad-ness and fear of what would happen if everyone around me knew my secret. I was and am a gay woman . . .

"There I was, a teenager, knowing that I felt the same pains, heard the same music, loved the same loves, and cried the same tears as all of my 'straight' friends. And yet I was receiving mes-sages from society that I was not normal, not okay."After Jennifer moved to Berkeley, Jim and Elise would often drive six hours to watch her play basketball, say hello for a little while, and then drive home. But even on these short visits, they sensed something amiss.

"A wall seemed to have grown between us," says Elise. "We'd go down there and then wouldn't have anything to talk to her about. And the phone calls were really excruciating. 'Hi, Mom and Dad, it's Jennifer'—and then, nothing. We felt we had to carry the whole load of the conversation, that we had to do all the talking."

During those excruciating silences, Jennifer often was silently mouthing into the telephone, "I'm gay, I'm gay." But she couldn't say it out loud except to her brother, Robert, then attending Oregon State University in Corvallis. Nevertheless, Jim and Elise were beginning to suspect the source of the unease. Jennifer had come out to most of her acquaintances on campus, and the Selfs noticed unmistakable signs when they visited.

"In a way," Elise says, "Jennifer did nothing to hide it." At the games it seemed there was "always a group of women around her." She lived with some other women in a house, and Elise recalls that at one point, "there was some kind of big split up—two of them had to get out of the house real quick, almost like a lovers' quarrel."

Finally, the parents asked Robert whether he thought Jennifer might be gay. Robert, respecting his sister's request for confidentiality, told them to ask Jennifer directly. Elise remembers the scene:

"It was after her sophomore year. We were all together, the four of us, and we sat her down in the family room. I said, 'Jennifer, there's a wall between us. Is there anything you want to tell us?' She said, 'No.' I said, 'Do you want me to make it easy for you?' She said, 'Yes.' I said, 'Are you gay?' She said, 'Yes.'

"And the wall came tumbling down. It was such a relief to have that secret out of the way. We cried. Then we could start dealing with all the feelings."

After what Elise describes as that "wonderful talk," however, the information was slow to extend beyond the family.

"I'm not proud to admit it," Elise says, "but quite frankly, my biggest concern at first, other than worry about Jennifer and her life, was, 'What are people going to think? What's my family going to think?'"

Then, by chance, Elise found P-FLAG.

While visiting Robert during "Mom's Weekend" at OSU in the spring of his senior year, Elise saw a sign announcing a meeting of the Corvallis P-FLAG group in a campus building. She grabbed Robert's hand and ran up the stairs and joined the meeting. For the first time, Elise was talking about Jennifer's gayness to people outside her immediate family.

"I cried and cried," she says. "It was the first time I had been with a group of people where I felt I could open up and talk about my daughter in a proud way, and be heard and be understood. It was a marvelous feeling."

Before she left the meeting, the leader gave her Candace Steele's phone number. Back home, Elise timidly dialed the number, and Candace answered.

"I could barely get it out," Elise says with a laugh. "Finally, I said it. 'I have a lesbian daughter.' And she said, 'Well, I have *two* lesbian daughters.' So it was wonderful."

Elise and Jim attended several P-FLAG meetings in Ashland. They had assumed that they were the only people in Grants Pass with a gay child—or who even knew anybody gay. But Candace gave them the names of gay and lesbian contacts there, and urged them to start a local P-FLAG group. The Selfs agreed to make an attempt, and planned a meeting in their home. Publicity was strictly word-of-mouth, but, to their surprise, ten people showed up. They continued to hold monthly meetings, and by 1993, a year-and-a-half later, the average attendance had grown to about twenty-five. "We've heard that gay people are everywhere," Jim says. "And if we can draw that many family members to P-FLAG meetings in a place like Grants Pass, I've got to believe it."

At the first meeting the Selfs had attended in Ashland, Jim had solemnly announced that he would never become an activist. But about the time the Selfs were hosting their first meeting, the OCA qualified their hate-ridden initiative for the ballot.

"Can you imagine it?" Jim asks. "You have just had your daughter come out to you, and then you sit and read that these people are lumping her with pedophiles and sadists. We were absolutely horrified. So all of a sudden, my resolve not to become an activist went into the trash can. We simply could not sit still and watch this hate campaign against people we loved."

For starters, Elise helped form a local human rights alliance that attracted a number of prominent local citizens and bridged the gap between the gay and mainstream communities. The alliance had been the dream of a group of closeted lesbians for whom the encouragement of a non-gay person provided the necessary impetus to make it a reality. The first meeting attracted eighty people—what Elise calls "a *very* large turnout for our little town." Nor was the meeting without drama. As Elise tells it:

"Jim and I stood up and came out publicly for the first time before so many local people. Then we went around the room. And every one of those eighty people shared some story about prejudice or discrimination they had experienced in their lives—because they were Jewish, or Catholic, or a person of color, or gay, or whatever. It was an incredible evening. It was a very intimate evening with eighty people, if you can imagine that. We never dreamed we could have an experience like that in Grants Pass."

The Selfs were proud of their role in creating this group to oppose the OCA, but they could not yet imagine coming out to the town as a whole. They even asked the meeting participants not to disclose Jennifer's secret. Jim's eighty-three-year-old mother also lived in Grants Pass, and they hadn't even told her

"So you can see how scared we still were," Elise says. As Jim notes, however, "The pressure was really mounting now. We've got my mother in town, and Elise's parents back East who don't know;

but we're also feeling an incredible urgency to get this message out, and to get out in the streets and start fighting the OCA."

The final push out of the closet was a call from Candace Steele. Opponents of Number 9 were putting together a voters' pamphlet that would include the names of P-FLAG parents. Would the Selfs allow their names to be used? Undecided, Jim and Elise called Jennifer in Berkeley.

"If you're ready to come out, I'm ready to have my name out there," was Jennifer's reply. "We need to fight this."

It was a momentous decision. For the first time, they would be out—not only in town, but statewide. "This was bigger than Grants Pass," Elise says. "But we said yes."

Now they *had* to inform the grandparents. They first told Jim's mother, Roberta Self. Jennifer couldn't get away from school to do it in person, but she nervously instructed her parents, "Ask Grandma if I still get the dishes."

She needn't have worried. Roberta Self's first reaction surprised and amused Jim and Elise. "Well," she snorted, "I feel better about the situation now. She's not down there on campus with those boys pawing all over her."

Next, the Selfs sent separate letters, one from Elise and Jim and one from Jennifer, to Elise's parents. Jennifer told her grandparents, "I am giving you a gift, and the gift is me and who I am."

"My folks called right away," Elise says. "My father left a message on the machine saying, 'We are with you. We read your letters several times. We have cried, and we love you and we love Jennifer.'

"But it hasn't been easy for them. They love Jennifer very much. They don't blame anyone. They understand that this is not a choice. But they have all that social conditioning we all have and they have to deal with that."

The Selfs' first live "media event" was a candlelight vigil for human rights on the steps of the county courthouse. Jim can now laugh at the fact that the report of his first public statement in support of gay rights, printed in the next day's newspaper, made it appear that he himself was gay: "I am only now learning how difficult it is to be openly gay in a heterosexual society."

But it was Elise who provided the emotional highlight of the evening. In proud and defiant tones, she read her personal tribute to her daughter:

> She cannot be reduced to statistics, polls, stereotypes, nicknames, prejudice, opinion.
>
> She is my child.
>
> I still have the same dreams. The details may have changed, but the dreams are the same:
>
> Of happiness, love, home, family, meaningful work.
>
> Because, you see, she is my child.
>
> She's not some monster to be feared, some pervert to be sneered at, some child molester or converter of adolescents.
>
> She is my child.
>
> She is warm and caring and sensitive and vulnerable and angry and sad, funny and human.
>
> Yes, she is my child.
>
> She didn't drop from another planet to cause destruction and mayhem.
>
> She came from love between her father and me.
>
> Yes, she is my child.
>
> You will not harm her if I can prevent it. You will not hurt her. She is my child.
>
> I join with every black mother, every Jewish mother, every Native American mother, every Hispanic mother, every Asian mother, every disabled child's mother, every gay child's mother, and every mother whose child has known hatred and prejudice.
>
> And I say they are our children, our very special, precious children.

But even as Elise's words stirred the hearts of those at the vigil, the vicious OCA campaign continued to pound away at them.

"Every single day we picked up the newspaper and read in effect about what a pervert our child was," Elise remembers. "It is difficult to convey the level of fear, of sheer intimidation, that the OCA's campaign had created."

Nevertheless, when a lesbian friend arranged for an interview by the Grants Pass *Daily Courier* with some gay residents, Jim and Elise agreed to join them. It was an opportunity to bring their family perspective more directly to the local townspeople. So, warily—uncertain what the tenor of the article might be—they endorsed the newspaper's plan to include a story about them in a series on Number 9.

On the morning the article was to appear, Jim and Elise awakened together, in near panic, at 4 AM. They sat rigidly in their living room, waiting for daybreak. Jim broke the tension—"Do you think we could go buy every *Courier* in town?" Eventually, they reassured themselves with the thought that the story would probably be buried on the community pages.

But when the *Courier* came out that afternoon, a huge picture of Elise, Jennifer, and Jim in a grinning, three-way embrace—with Elise sporting a tee shirt reading "Straight but Not Narrow"—loomed from every newsstand in town. "Local Family Loves Its Lesbian Daughter" blared the front-page banner above the picture.

The story was positive. It described the Selfs as "an all-American family sparked by high achievement." It contrasted Jennifer's public stardom with the inner tumult of her high school years, and told of the difficult experience of coming out to her family and the ensuing family closeness. It described the Selfs' P-FLAG experience. It quoted Robert saying of his parents, "I'm proud of them." And it concluded with a quote from Jim: "People who have gays or lesbians in their family do believe in traditional values. They do love their families."

The article infuriated local members of the OCA, and for two weeks, the *Courier* was picketed by protesters complaining that the newspaper was unfair to the organization.

"Can you believe it?" Jim still marvels. "They turned *themselves* into the victims! They said they were being discriminated against because the newspaper had the nerve to print this story. I'm not sure what they wanted. Maybe a story about people who *didn't* love their daughter?"

The article also triggered heavy response from across the political and religious spectrums. The *Courier* received waves of letters to the editor and the Selfs were deluged with telephone calls, letters, and comments from passers-by.

Many of the responses were angry and vicious. The Selfs received a spate of hate letters; and it was the edge-of-violence tone of many of them that led Jim to get a gun. And the virulence of the OCA campaign seemed to have no limits. One pro-amendment flier, never renounced by the OCA, actually called for castrating and executing all gays. The "perverted gay lobby will be defeated," it said, "only when all Christians unite" to "implement God's methods to exterminate homosexuals . . . Execution . . . Castration . . . Imprisonment."

But there were compensations. For months after the article was published, people stopped the Selfs on the street to tell them, "Thanks for the article; I have someone gay in my family." Nearly a year later, addressing delegates to a national P-FLAG convention, Jim choked back tears as he read a letter that the family received in 1992. It was from Lorenz "Lefty" Schultz, pastor of Newman Church, and more than one hundred members of the congregation.

> Dear Jim, Elise, and Jennifer,
>
> In the past couple of years, you and your family have been through an extraordinary journey together. In the interest of creating a human community where understanding, compassion, and tolerance can abide instead of intolerance and fear, you have taken some very great risks in sharing your story with the whole community. We suspect that your willingness to share such depth

and vulnerability may have exposed you to the hatred and big-otry that represents a darker side of our community.

As a congregation, we are not all of a single mind on the issue of homosexuality; but in our differences we can unite in affirm-ing the importance of communication, caring, love, growth, truth-telling, the ability to rejoice in laughter, and to share the wellspring of tears and fundamental values which lie at the heart of deep and precious family relationships.

We hear much rhetoric these days about family values and family relationships. You and your family live and embody those family values.

As members and friends of Newman Church, we reach out to you in love and caring. You need to know that you represent the best that we have to offer this community. We are pleased to call you neighbors and friends.

During the frenzied final weeks of the campaign, hundreds of advertisements were placed in the *Courier* by both sides of the Number 9 controversy. On the final weekend before the vote, one full-page ad featured a letter from Jennifer addressed to "Dear Citizens of Josephine County." In it, she recounted her youthful years in Grants Pass, described the hardship created by negative public attitudes toward homosexuality, and pleaded for under-standing and tolerance.

She realized, she wrote, that many people held religious beliefs that precluded them from accepting homosexuality. But to those, she said, "I pose the question, what's the danger, the evil, in accept-ing and loving someone you don't understand or agree with? Aren't these the ideals by which Jesus Christ lived life?" She urged them, "Make a vote for love, acceptance, and education, and vote no on Ballot Measure 9."

Significantly, and probably crucially, similar pleas were being made by numerous nonfundamentalist churches. The Ecumenical Ministries of Oregon, representing seventeen denominations and more than two thousand congregations, correctly described the initiative as promoting "a climate of bigotry, hatred, and intimidation." And in what many considered a landmark event, Oregon's Catholic bishops joined the "No on 9" forces, denouncing the measure as "potentially harmful and discriminatory."

On election day, Number 9 was defeated 57 to 43 percent. In Portland, three thousand people at a post-election rally gave a rousing ovation to P-FLAGger Marge Work, a tireless "No on 9" campaigner. Presented with a certificate from the gay community designating her as "our P-FLAG Mom for loving us unconditionally," she told the crowd, "It's a mother's prerogative to brag about her children. You've honored me with the title, so I'm going to claim the prerogative. I'm so proud of you, everyone of you. You're fine the way you are. You are loved. And we are here for you."

Ominously, however, the victory was achieved only because of heavy majorities in Portland. Rural counties approved of the measure by resounding margins that ran as high as two to one. In Josephine County, 58 percent of the voters endorsed the measure.

The OCA was heartened by the amendment's heavy support in rural areas, as well as by the passage of a somewhat tamer anti-gay measure in Colorado the same day. Within months, the OCA was sponsoring "Baby Number 9's"—local ordinances banning civil rights protections for gays—in the twenty counties that had favored the statewide measure. One of them, its wording patterned on the Colorado model, became Proposition 17-1 on Josephine County's 1993 primary ballot; and the Selfs once again found themselves in battle.

Two months before the election, the entire family took a well-earned breather; they joined some 2,000 P-FLAGgers and an estimated 750,000 others in a massive turnout for the 1993 march on Washington for gay rights. When Jim and Elise returned to face the Proposition 17-1 campaign, they wrote an op-ed piece for the *Courier*; it described their "inspirational and emotional weekend" in Washington and drew lessons for the voters of Josephine County.

They had cried, they wrote, when they stood before the Lincoln Memorial and read Lincoln's words about a nation "dedicated to the proposition that all men are created equal." They cried again when they walked along the Vietnam War Memorial, read the names of Americans killed, and wondered which of them were gay men or lesbians. And they cried yet again, they wrote, at the new Holocaust Memorial Museum: "It was not insignificant that the Museum opened at the time of the march. It was chilling to remember what the Nazis did to gays and lesbians, while at the same time reading the signs of some who came to protest the March: DEATH TO ALL FAGS!"

It was also during the final weeks of the Proposition 17-1 campaign that Jennifer received from her grandmother a gift more valuable by far than the family dishes. A letter penned and signed by Roberta Self in her precise handwriting was mailed to fifteen thousand Josephine County voters. In it, after declaring her love for her granddaughter, she wrote, "What they [the OCA] are really doing is trying to hurt my granddaughter. They are trying to hurt so many of our precious children."

The letter became known throughout the county as "the grandmother letter." Jim says, "So here's my eighty-three-year-old Southern Baptist, prim, proper Virginian mother, who prides herself on being a very private person, now being a community celebrity. For about ten days, she was absolutely deluged with telephone calls." Newspapers ran stories about Roberta Self and her letter, and it was the topic of a heated two-hour discussion on a local fundamentalist radio talk show.

One columnist wrote about the "swarm of angry phone calls" Roberta had received from Bible-quoting critics, and lauded her calm response. "Her well-worn Bible speaks of a God of understanding and compassion for all, not one of intolerance and hatred to those who may be different," he wrote. "Our world needs more such grandmothers."

Still, the Self family message was no match for ingrained stereotypes and the slick, moneyed campaign of the anti-gay forces. On June 28, 1993, Proposition 17-1 passed by an overwhelming margin.

Elise, drawing an analogy to the Rogue River, says that in the family's journey in support of their daughter, "We have hit white water—and it can be scary." But they paddle on because, as Elise puts it, "We now know that there are people on the banks cheering us on. And there are a lot of others who have taken to their boats and gotten in the river with us. So we feel a lot safer now because we know we're not alone."

Moreover, she says, the journey has been "an incredibly liberating experience" for the entire family. "Coming out has been an enormous relief. I feel so free. I don't care anymore what anybody else might think."

That, it seems, is one of the rewards of true courage.

7

•

The Radical Challenge

Ground Zero for the Holy War

fter visiting Colorado Springs in 1892, Katharine Lee Bates
wrote the text of the national hymn "America the Beautiful."
Millions of visitors there have since been similarly
awestruck by the blue-skied grandeur of Pikes Peak and the
Rockies' magnificent Front Range.

At the hundredth anniversary celebration of her song, considerable attention was paid to a long-standing conjecture that Bates,
a professor of English literature at Wellesley College, was a lesbian.
If so, she would have no longer felt comfortable in that land of
spacious skies and purple mountains' majesty.

Now, the amber grain is blown by the winds of moral zealotry.
The fruited plain has sprouted dozens of conservative Christian
ministries that have proclaimed Colorado Springs "Ground Zero
for the War between God and Satan." And to the crusaders, the
forces of Satan are led by lesbians and gay men.

In 1991, Coloradoans for Family Values (CFV), a group founded and chaired by local car dealer Will Perkins, broadened the
anti-gay battlefield to the entire state. They sought to outlaw civil
rights protections for lesbians and gay men, and their vehicle was
a constitutional initiative, Amendment Number 2.

The bitter, destructive campaign would profoundly affect families throughout the state. Among them were those of two Colorado Springs couples, the McGeehans and the Frums, and a state official living in a Denver suburb, Pat Romero.

Eva and Hugh McGeehan were lifelong liberal-minded Easterners, attracted in retirement by Colorado Springs's scenic beauty. Bonnie and Buzz Frum were personal friends of Will Perkins, fundamentalist Christians who ultimately honored a different set of family values than did Perkins. Romero, director of human resources for the state Department of Education, would find herself side-by-side with Colorado's governor quelling a 1992 election-night riot.

The McGeehans were lured to Colorado Springs by the area's outward charms, but suffered culture shock once there. Now, six years later, having helped to found a P-FLAG chapter and nursing it through infancy as its co-president, Eva thinks the move might have been fated. "Sometimes I think this is where I was supposed to be."

Before the McGeehans were married, Eva had worked in New York City as a publicity director for a line of ladies' shoes; and in the world of fashion, she met many openly gay men. Hugh, a World War II Air Force pilot and Cornell University graduate, worked in corporate management in five different eastern cities; he had come to accept people as he found them. So when Patrick, their second child and first son, told them he was gay, their principal concern was for his well-being. Their three other children were equally accepting. Patrick's homosexuality was a non-issue to the McGeehans—until Eva and Hugh moved to Colorado Springs.

For fifteen years prior to Hugh's retirement and two years after, the McGeehans lived in Reston, Virginia. Then in August 1989, during the muggy Virginia summer, they visited daughter Mollie, a student at the University of Colorado at Colorado Springs. They were captivated by the area's natural beauty and the dry, pleasant climate. Ten days after arriving in town for what had been planned as a vacation, they bought a house.

A year later, relocated to the pleasant home within eyeshot of Pikes Peak and the red-rocked Garden of the Gods, they savored the agreeable weather. But they were soon to learn that the social climate was much less hospitable. Their new home, they discovered, was a wellspring of moral vigilantism.

Colorado Springs basks in nearly perpetual sunlight, sprinkled along the steeply rising foothills beneath the majestic Rocky Mountains. For decades, its economy rested almost entirely upon tourism. But After World War II, the Pentagon's missile-tracking nerve center was installed inside nearby Cheyenne Mountain, and the Air Force Academy was built on the city's northern edge. In the 1980s, drawn perhaps by the blend of scenic beauty and conservative military tradition, rightist Christian organizations migrated in increasing numbers.

By the early 1990s, when the McGeehans were settling in there, the ministries employed thousands of people; and fundamentalist religion had become a staple of the city's economic base. (In 1992, a single one of these organizations, Focus on the Family, reportedly earned $90 million distributing magazines, books, cassettes, and videos to parents and teachers throughout the country.) Churches dotted the landscape, and the five Christian radio stations dominated the airwaves. The fifty-four church-related organizations in Colorado Springs gave the city one of the world's greatest concentrations of such bodies. And on December 25, 1994, a *Washington Post* article on the city reported complaints about "crosses on the uniforms of some police officers . . . evolution omitted from a science curriculum . . . and fear being expressed that 'rainbow' is a code word for a gay agenda." News commentator Bill Moyers has observed, "Some folks . . . now refer to the town as Vatican West."

Shortly after the McGeehans moved in, Eva attended a religious retreat sponsored by a nearby Catholic church. It was there that she had her first brush with the kind of bias that within months would give rise to Amendment Number 2. On the first evening of the three-day session, she was stunned to hear a group of women engaged in a vicious round of verbal gay-bashing. (Sample rhetoric: "I hate them all. They give babies AIDS.") Having come for spiritual solace only to find its antithesis, Eva almost left that first evening.

A sympathetic priest talked Eva into staying, and the next morning she spoke publicly for the first time about her son's homosexuality. She told the women about Patrick, about other gay people she had known, and about the love she had witnessed in a gay community banded together to meet the AIDS crisis. Recalling the event, she reflects, "The people in my church talk about the Holy Spirit, but I never really understood it. Well, I think the Holy Spirit wrote my talk. I can't believe it to this day."

Her comments were warmly received. She saw tears on the faces of some women. One of the prior evening's gay-bashers apologized to her for what she had said. And Eva's words triggered a grateful response from another woman, Perey Riley, who had a lesbian daughter. The two sat on a staircase sipping wine, exchanging stories; the friendship born there flowered into the organization of a Colorado Springs chapter of P-FLAG.

First, they found a support group that had formed largely in response to the accelerating anti-gay tension as Perkins mounted the petition drive that would eventually place Number 2 on the ballot. Eva and Perey then helped the group affiliate with P-FLAG, and Eva was elected co-president of the new chapter.

In the charged local atmosphere, Hugh and Eva now stood out among families with gay members, who for the most part were maintaining a low profile. A few of Eva's letters were even published by the city's daily newspaper, a devout editorial supporter of Number 2. In one, she wrote: "Yes, gays and lesbians do have parents, sisters and brothers and friends who love them. . . . They do not appreciate having loved ones regarded as abominations or polluters of the earth. Nor do they appreciate so-called 'Christians' dooming their souls to hell. . . . P-FLAG members have their own family values."

A local columnist also wrote about the McGeehans and the fledgling P-FLAG chapter. The column included an account of how Hugh had spoken about Patrick at a reunion of his all-male Catholic high school in New York City. Although he attended the reunions every five years, and returnees were always asked to report on what had been happening in their lives, he had never mentioned having a gay son. This time, though, when it came his turn, he stood and said, "I'm going to talk to you about something I should have talked to you about five years ago, but couldn't." He told them about his pride in Patrick, a researcher for *National Geographic Magazine*, and to his surprise received a standing ovation.

For a time, the P-FLAG meetings in Colorado Springs drew no more than ten or twelve people. But the numbers grew as the meetings provided a haven from the increasingly ugly local mood. Gays and lesbians were reporting a stream of menacing telephone calls, broken windows, and even death threats.

The amendment backers purported to be carrying the word of God, but their campaign message often seemed devilish. It had two fear-based themes. One was designed to energize the faithful by painting dark visions of homosexual demons out to recruit innocent youth. ("We don't want homosexuals to come into our homes with our own taxpayer money and take our little children," snarled one Number 2 supporter.) The other exploited the growing middle-class resentment of perceived excesses of earlier civil rights movements; it warned, irrationally but effectively, that unless Number 2 passed, gays would soon have special rights based on affirmative action quota systems. As Perkins put it, gay people were saying, "Because of what we're doing in the bedroom, we want special protections, special rights." The spurious nature of both arguments would be more fully demonstrated by events after the election.

*   *   *

One of the Colorado Springs families caught in the political cross-fire were the Frums, themselves longtime fundamentalist Christians. In mid-1991, about the time the anti-gay initiative was picking up steam, the Frums learned that two of their children were gay: eighteen-year-old Christie and seventeen-year-old Matt came out to their parents simultaneously. (The Frums also have another son, David, then seven.)

Fortunately for Bonnie and Buzz, Christie and Matt had heard of P-FLAG and suggested that all four attend a meeting together. Eva McGeehan says the Frums' despair that first day will remain in her memory forever.

P-FLAG was then meeting in a psychotherapist's office, which was barely large enough to accommodate the four Frums and the eight or ten others. "Buzz couldn't even speak, couldn't even say the words," Eva remembers. "Through her tears, Bonnie was barely able to get out the story about just learning they had a gay son *and* a gay daughter." In a little more than a year, though, they would travel from stunned new parents to co-presidents of an enlarged Colorado Springs P-FLAG chapter; and they would go head-to-head over Number 2 in their own living room with Will Perkins.

Like Mary Griffith (see Chapter 5), the Frums attended a fundamentalist Presbyterian church. But unlike her, they were able to do what Griffith wished she had done: they listened to their parental instincts and conscience rather than to the dogma of their church.

Bonnie came forward and accepted Christ when she was fourteen, and after high school she spent four years in a Bible school and with an affiliated organization that ran youth camps and teen clubs. Buzz was raised a Catholic and spent six months in a Trappist monastery before deciding that he did not have the gift of celibacy; he left the church and enthusiastically embraced Bonnie's evangelism after they were married.

For two decades, they remained devoted to evangelical Christian life. They led neighborhood Bible studies, taught Sunday school, and immersed themselves in the doings of their church. In the 1970s, Buzz even served as director of development for an international organization he describes as the evangelical counterpart of the World Council of Churches. (He is now a stockbroker.) And Christie and Matt, during their junior high years, chose to attend an even stricter church than that of their parents.

To an outside observer in early 1991, Bonnie, Buzz, and their three children might have seemed a sort of ultra-religious Cleaver family. They lived twelve doors away from Buzz's parents on an attractive, tree-lined street of substantial middle class homes. Life appeared to be following a carefully defined, predictable path. In fact, though, Bonnie and Buzz were already feeling somewhat restless about their church's brand of Christianity. Even before Christie and Matt came out to them, they were beginning to question an unrelentingly literal interpretation of the Bible and the dogmatism of certain church teachings. But caution remained their byword. In Colorado Springs, after all, challenges to fundamentalist Christian doctrine are hardly *de rigueur*.

Meanwhile, Matt had become aware of his homosexuality when he was eleven or twelve; Christie realized hers a few years later. Matt suffered torments similar to those of Bobby Griffith. "I was constantly praying to God to change me," he says. "I would cry in bed at night." In high school, he came out first to a friend who was gay, and later to other pals. Although his closest friends were accepting, he was regularly taunted and threatened by others. One such incident came to the attention of the principal, who blamed the victim. "Look in the mirror," the principal told Matt. "If you weren't this way, it wouldn't happen to you."

Bonnie and Buzz sensed something was wrong. They had always felt close to both children, but now could feel the children pulling away. So in the spring of 1991, the parents insisted that they all see a professional counselor. Christie and Matt had only recently come out to each other, and had pledged not to tell their parents. But during just the second counseling session, they found themselves disclosing what it was that had been disrupting family rapport.

The revelation put Bonnie and Buzz into shock. "We went home from that session and cried all night," Bonnie recalls. "I think I cried for nearly a whole year, off and on."

It was time for a phenomenon not uncommon among P-FLAG families—some parent-child role reversal.

"The kids were wonderful," Bonnie says. "They gave us lots of time to adjust. Matt said, 'Mom, it's taken me many years to get used to the fact that I'm gay. I can give you and Dad all the time you need.' They didn't get offended that we were bawling all the time."

The children were aware of P-FLAG through a local gay hotline; and within a month the four attended that first meeting remembered so vividly by Eva McGeehan. "When it came our turn to speak," Bonnie says, "Buzz started bawling and asked me to introduce us. So I started to say, 'We have two gay kids.'" Here, she breaks into a wail as she imitates that earlier performance: "'Oh, we have two! Two!'

"We thought, this is just too much. But the people at P-FLAG were wonderful. They let us be where we were. They didn't say, 'Oh, your kids are wonderful, you should be happy.' They let us cry and not be very happy about it."

The parents read several books about homosexuality. In one, Bonnie read that "someday you'll rejoice over having a gay child." "I thought, 'I'll never rejoice over this.' I told that to Matt and he said, 'Mom, I don't know that I'll ever rejoice.'"

All four Frums now acknowledge, however, that their journey has brought, if not rejoicing, some important rewards and personal growth.

For Bonnie and Buzz, one result was a final break from their church, a strong backer of Number 2. They were upset when friends there told them Christie and Matt needed to see a psychiatrist—"that something was wrong and it was sinful, not what God wants." Their patience finally snapped when the couple who were David's godparents insisted they had to tell the youngster that his brother and sister were sinful. "They saw it as an obligation as his godparents to do *that* to our little David," Bonnie says, shaking her head sadly.

So to Bonnie and Buzz, the fundamentalist party line on homosexuality was found wanting. However, their sentiments would not prevail on election day 1992. Number 2 passed statewide by a 53 to 47 percent margin—and in Colorado Springs by a landslide two to one. Whether the courts will allow it to go into effect remains uncertain. But, whatever its fate as law, the measure has trailed a wake of anger and discord.

And in Denver, on election night, but for Pat Romero, it might have produced a riot.

Denver boasts one of P-FLAG's largest and most active chapters, several hundred strong, and for a time in the 1980s housed its national office. Pat Romero had been a member for some years before the advent of Number 2; but it was the vitriol of that campaign that converted her into an activist. She became a key opposition figure, a familiar face and voice on television and radio and at "No on 2" rallies.

The defining moment of her commitment to gay rights, however, did not come until the night before the election. She had been standing alone beside a busy street, waving a "No on 2" sign as evening commuters passed, when a car skidded across two lanes of traffic to pull up beside her. The driver spat on her, shouted, "Fuck you, dyke!" and roared away.

It was a traumatic experience. "I never really appreciated the terror our children face until that moment," she says.

Romero's gay son, Mick Barnhardt, is an architectural engineer whose relationship with Mike Bieri, a systems analyst, is in its twelfth year. But it was concern for her youngest child, Michelle, that first led her to P-FLAG eight years ago, shortly after Michelle started first grade in their middle class, mostly white neighborhood.

Michelle came home that first week of school, parrotting other children, and told Pat that "Mexicans and blacks are ugly."

"Do you think April is ugly?" Pat asked. April, an African American, had been Michelle's best friend in day care. Michelle promptly replied, "No."

"Do you think I'm ugly?" Pat asked. "No."

"Well," Pat said, "I'm Mexican and you're half-Mexican."

Then, Pat recalls, "Right on the heels of that, she came home talking about 'homos.' I said, 'Wait a minute, Michelle.' And she said, 'Momma, don't tell me I'm half homo, too!'"

Pat felt that Michelle had always accepted Bieri as a brother-in-law just as she had the husbands of her two older sisters, but now Pat sought out P-FLAG to help Michelle adjust to the homophobic atmosphere at school. Her subsequent activism in the fight against Number 2 seemed for her a natural step.

Despite strong financial backing and disciplined fundamentalist support for the measure, pre-election polls predicted the amendment's defeat. So on the evening of November 3, 1992, Pat joined several thousand of the measure's opponents in Denver's Mammoth Gardens for an expected victory celebration. But joy turned to shock as the "yes" votes mounted to the ultimate 53 percent majority. Many voters, it seemed, had simply misled the pollsters.

About five hundred of the "No on 2" mourners, Romero among them, hastily put together a large banner reading, "Forgive them, Father, for they know not what they do." Holding it high, they marched to the hotel where Democrats were celebrating the election of Bill Clinton.

By the time the crowd reached the hotel, the shock had worn off and was replaced by anger. The crowd became unruly, even rocking and threatening to tip over a police car that had responded for crowd control. For a while, riot threatened. With one other woman, Romero climbed up on a planter and pleaded with the protesters to stay calm. Then Governor Roy Romer and Denver Mayor Wellington Webb came out of the hotel. They joined Romero on the planter, and the crowd finally quieted when Governor Romer promised to meet with them the following morning.

"I was standing right in front of the governor," Romero remembers. "I could feel him gripping my shoulder and I thought, 'My God, he's scared.' Then I realized he was just afraid of falling off that planter."

The next morning, an Associated Press photo of Pat and the second woman on the planter appeared in newspapers around the country; and she received a print from the photographer with a note, "Thank God you two women were there."

The night after the election, 7,000 people turned out for a candlelight vigil on the courthouse steps. Pat was one of the speakers, and was greeted by waves of shouts, "We love you, Mom." Mick, in the crowd, turned to one of the shouters near him and said proudly, "She's *my* Mom."

In the aftermath of the fractious campaign, the falseness and hypocrisy of Number 2's strongest arguments came clear.

A post-election study of child sex abuse cases in Colorado showed that less than one percent were committed by a homosexual perpetrator. In other words, gays weren't even committing their statistical share of such abuse, much less posing any special threat, as charged by Number 2's backers.

The hypocrisy of the special rights argument also became apparent. In 1993, a group of Colorado Springs businesspeople, alarmed about the possible adverse economic fallout from the national publicity surrounding Number 2, proposed a compromise measure. It would have banned both anti-gay discrimination *and* any provisions that might create quotas or other special rights for homosexuals. Tellingly, the proposal was quickly pronounced unacceptable by the very groups that had so vehemently rung the special rights alarm in the first case.

The implementation of Amendment 2 was stalled by the courts after a lawsuit was filed by a group that included Aspen resident Martina Navratilova. A lower court handed down an immediate injunction against enforcement of the measure, and the state supreme court later declared the amendment unconstitutional. The case is under review by the U.S. Supreme Court; if upheld by that body, the decision could put an end to the kinds of initiatives seen in Oregon and Colorado in 1992.

The immediate effect of the injunction, however was a violent anti-gay backlash. Newspapers reported that a Colorado Springs psychotherapist whose only apparent failing was to display a bumper sticker reading "Celebrate Diversity" was knocked unconscious and had her home spray-painted with slogans such as "Seek God," "Stop Evil," and "Repent." The front window of another home was smashed, apparently because the family had placed a "Hate Free Home" sticker on it. A man who made a gay-friendly statement in a newspaper man-in-the-street interview received more than a dozen hate calls. "They called me a faggot, damned me to hell, and told me to read the Bible," he reported.

Meanwhile, the Frums spent a few hours in their living room sharing views with old friend Will Perkins. The talk "didn't change anything," Buzz says, "but we tried to help him see he didn't have a corner on the market as to a Christian perspective on sexuality." Buzz told Perkins he particularly objected to the phrase "militant homosexual agenda" that appeared so often in anti-gay campaigns. "Every time you say that," Buzz told Perkins, "think about Bonnie and me, because we're espousing this agenda you say is militant." They also told Perkins they resented the attempt by the amendment's backers to usurp the family values banner. They said they are honoring the family values they grew up with in their own traditional families: love, respect, compassion, integrity, and mutual support.

Perkins told them he regretted the choice of his organization's name because he realized that others, such as the Frums, are also family-oriented. But his words rang hollow when he took his campaign nationwide. A notebook called *The Colorado Model* was distributed around the country, at $95 a copy, to groups hoping to repeat the organization's success elsewhere. (Among its suggestions: Find spokespersons along the model of "amiable, jovial, self-deprecating" Will Perkins, whom the booklet says "personifies an uncanny recreation of Ronald Reagan's rhetorical attributes.") In some instances, CFV helped other anti-gay campaigns with outright cash contributions. In 1993, for example, Cincinnati voters approved a city measure modeled on Number 2, and 70 percent of the funds for the proponents' campaign were reportedly supplied by Perkins's group. And Colorado-style initiatives were launched in eleven states in 1994. (Only two, in Oregon and Idaho, made it to the November ballot. Each of them was defeated, but by margins so narrow as to encourage anti-gay forces for the future.)

The Colorado campaign, by putting parents on notice about the genuine threats to their children, triggered a growth in P-FLAG membership and activity. In Denver, where the average pre-election meeting attendance had been about 125 people, sessions now drew up to 175. Requests to the chapter's speaker bureau rose from 100 in 1991 to 140 in 1992. In Pueblo, P-FLAG president Nancy Martin was one of a group of P-FLAGgers who helped put together the gay community's first local organization, named Pueblo After Two. By the following summer, in a city where lesbians and gay men had before kept an extremely low profile, Pueblo After Two staffed a booth at the annual Colorado State Fair. And P-FLAG chapters throughout the state reported swelling attendance and membership.

In Colorado Springs, when the Frums took over as P-FLAG co-presidents in early 1993, average meeting attendance had already

grown fourfold and forced the group out of the cramped thera-
pist's office into a room in a church. But continued influx soon
demanded another move, this time to a building that could
accommodate the up to seventy people now regularly attending
meetings. This growth has occurred despite the fact that the
charged local atmosphere still prevents advertising meeting locations: "We don't want to take a chance on parents being accosted
going to meetings," Bonnie says.

The Frums, who have joined a Methodist church receptive to
their support of their gay children, lament the injection of religion
into gay rights issues. Perkins continues to deny that CFV is reli-
giously oriented, but the group's zealous executive director, Kevin
Tebedo, seems not to have gotten the message. In a PBS report
about the fundamentalist fervor in Colorado Springs he declaims,
"We talk about separation of church and state. Ladies and gentle-
men, Jesus Christ *is* the King of Kings and the Lord of Lords; and
He said that all power and authority were given unto Him. *That* is
political." (A Colorado newspaper credited Tebedo with another
startling statement, to the effect that nearly every newspaper
reporter in Colorado has a red phone—a direct hotline to "militant homosexual organizations"–in the desk drawer.)

Fundamentalist forces gave much of the credit for Number 2's
passage to the outspoken support of Bill McCartney, a state idol
who coached Colorado University's football team to a national
championship. During the campaign, McCartney led 25,000 men in
a massive religious rally, a veritable paean to patriarchy, in the university football stadium. At a highly publicized press conference,
McCartney stood before the university logo and heatedly called
homosexuality "an abomination of God." The president of the university reprimanded McCartney for using his official capacity to
further his personal politics; but the publicity generated by the
series of events was one of the amendment's most important
boosts.

All this provided the Frums with some wry amusement. The

"abomination" language, so dear to anti-gay forces everywhere, stems from Leviticus. But the same book also lays down taboos against eating shellfish, wearing cloth of mixed fabrics, and—touching the skin of a dead pig. Stealing a line from one of Colorado Springs's progressive ministers, the Reverend Jim White of the United Church of Christ, Buzz intones in mock seriousness: "Oh, oh! There goes football at CU!"

Neither irony nor the crusaders' sloppy Biblical scholarship could slow the anti-gay cause. But one post-election development provided gay supporters with a new voice in Colorado Springs. This was the founding of a progressive weekly newspaper, the *Independent*, which among other things became an outlet for the views of P-FLAG members. A 1994 issue carried a statement by three sets of parents—Ed and Gerda Fletcher, Leo and Linda Bohack, and Bill and Pat Pfeiffer—that could well serve as a general manifesto of the organization. In particular, it took dead aim at what it called anti-gay "pseudo-family groups" that employ battleground terms ("Holy War" or "God's warfare") in describing their cause:

> We submit that declaring war on the people we love is not a family value. And we challenge any organization or individual who uses the term "family values" for such profane ends. . . .
>
> P-FLAG parents the world over know that the great majority of our gay and lesbian children—just like our heterosexual children—are upstanding citizens, hard working, contributing members of society. They are loving family members, spiritually strong and morally responsible. They have enriched our lives and broadened our horizons. Quite simply, they are a blessing bestowed by God and we love them just as they are. Their value to us and to society is not debatable.
>
> We would like to reassure young gays and lesbians of whatever religious background that just because they have a different sexual orientation, they are not evil or "morally bankrupt" or

pathological. We also want to assure their families that there *is* another voice in this community which can provide valid information about homosexuality and offer guidance away from prejudice, condemnation, and irrational fear.

Keeping families together is the mission of P-FLAG. Our family values stress education, understanding, acceptance, and support, but most of all, *love*, thereby empowering all our children— straight and gay—to lead happy and productive lives.

The heritage of Katharine Lee Bates has dimmed but not died in Colorado Springs. Declarations of moral warfare notwithstanding, sensitivity of spirit has not wholly withered in the land of spacious skies and purple mountains' majesty.

8

◆

Parents Speak Out

Most P-FLAG parents, unlike those described in Chapters 6 and 7, do not become activists, and no one in the organization is pressed to do so. P-FLAG's overriding aim is to provide a source of comfort for family and friends of gay people. It follows that the nature of anyone's participation is strictly a matter of personal choice.

What has nonetheless converted thousands of parents to activism is their distress at society's unfair treatment of their children. They work daily for their children's civil rights, largely without fanfare, in a variety of forums: in their churches, in private meetings with municipal and school officials, before school boards and city councils, in state capitals, and on Capitol Hill. They appear on radio and television talk shows, write letters to newspapers, meet with local media managers, and are frequent subjects of print feature stories. Every issue of P-FLAG's quarterly newsletter, *The PFLAGpole*, carries scores of items about members engaged in such activities in cities and hamlets across the country. Here are some examples:

- In Massachusetts, with the support of conservative Republican governor William Weld, members help bring about the nation's first commission on gay and lesbian youth and the first law to protect public school students from anti-gay discrimination. The commission head specifically acknowledges P-FLAG's importance in the developments, and describes the leadership of Regional Director Jean Genasci as "an inspiration."

- In eight states, P-FLAGgers are among the lead lobbyists in successful campaigns to enact statewide civil rights protections for gays. In other states, members continue to work for similar measures.

- In municipalities around the country—including New Orleans; Portland, Oregon; Portland, Maine; Denver; Montgomery County, Maryland, and others—P-FLAGgers play important roles in achieving local anti-discrimination protections.

- In San Jose, Ann Davidson and other P-FLAGgers join with a local PTA in staging a conference to educate parents and teachers to the problems faced by gay youth. The conference becomes a model for similar conferences elsewhere in the country.

- Around the nation, P-FLAG groups initiate library projects to make informative books about homosexuality—including those directed to parents of gays—generally available. One such project in Nebraska, spurred by Eileen Durgin-Clinchard of Omaha, places a set of eight books in each of sixty-eight state libraries. Another, initiated by Tom Sauerman, supplies sets of books to all of Philadelphia's fifty-three libraries.

- In scores of localities, P-FLAG speaker bureaus send representatives to churches, schools, colleges, and community groups to explain P-FLAG's aims and philosophy. (Many of the campus appearances are before organizations of gay students, which are forming rapidly at most colleges.)

- In Appleton, Wisconsin, members Harriet and George Bruyn launch a sensitivity training program for police recruits. In Washington, D.C., Beverley Southerland heads a similar initiative, and other P-FLAGgers work with police in New

Orleans and sheriff's deputies in Greenville, South Carolina.
- In Phoenix, members Ray Grove and Bunny and George Tarquinio help convince the city's library advisory board to deny a Concerned Women of America demand that certain gay-friendly books be banned. In Fairfax County, Virginia, P-FLAG parents are among those who successfully urge county supervisors not to ban a gay newspaper from local libraries.
- In Washington, D.C., Charles Wood—a retired Navy lieutenant commander and now an Episcopal minister—testifies before a House committee against the military's anti-gay policy. Other parents—including Pat Thorne, mother of Navy Lieutenant Tracy Thorne (see below)—meet with their representatives on the issue at home and on Capitol Hill.
- Throughout the country, P-FLAGgers address local, regional, and national religious bodies, playing significant roles in the glacial process of warming in church attitudes toward homosexuality. (See Chapter 9.)
- After a visit from P-FLAG constituents, Ohio Representative Thomas Sawyer writes Akron Chapter President Ann Beebe that P-FLAG is key to changing public attitudes.
- In Tucson, P-FLAGger and clinical psychologist Jean Baker, former president of the Arizona Psychological Association, speaks regularly to groups of teachers, counselors, psychologists, and social workers about the social cost of homophobia.
- In Grand Junction, Colorado, ex-Governor Richard Lamm is the keynoter of a conference largely organized by P-FLAG member Judy Weinberg to search for a middle ground between liberals and conservatives on social issues.
- In Tyler, Texas, following the murder of a gay man there, a "Stop the Hate" rally is addressed by Dallas chapter president Pat Stone and by Regional Director Sandra Moore. They call on parents to make the safety of their gay children a higher priority than "fear of what the neighbors might think."

- In Washington, D.C., a P-FLAG couple are among the speakers at a National Press Club announcement of President Clinton's denunciation of the 1994 wave of anti-gay initiatives sponsored by the radical right.

In these and countless other ways, P-FLAG members work tirelessly to mitigate ill-informed prejudice. The stories of two families—the Potters of Oregon and the Thornes of Florida—reflect the commitment of P-FLAG parents seeking a better world for their loved ones.

The Supercop

You don't have to be a gay activist to recognize that anti-gay attitudes and rhetoric result in a significant amount of crime. Killings, beatings, and harassment of gay Americans are common fare on police blotters. In Texas recently, eight hate-inspired killings of gay men were recorded in less than eighteen months.

In 1994, nevertheless, the Clinton administration shunned a top law enforcement official because he openly opposes anti-gay discrimination. That's like firing a medical director for backing DPT shots; hatred endangers public order in the same way diphtheria and tetanus threaten public health.

The official in question was Tom Potter, Portland, Oregon's former chief of police, who had been slated to head a 1994 Crime Bill program adding 100,000 officers to the nation's streets. Potter is a supercop with a lustrous record of achievement. However, he withdrew his name from consideration for the federal post when the Justice Department quailed at his record of support for gay rights, fearing it could hamper his effectiveness with conservative police chiefs.

Potter agreed to serve as a consultant to the program. But its command post was deprived of his special brand of administrative and crime-fighting savvy—one more casualty of common bigotry.

And the real victim of this bureaucratic timidity was a nation beset by escalating prejudice, lawlessness, and violence.

One afternoon in early 1993, Tom and Katie Potter sat together in Tom's fifteenth-floor Police Bureau office, he in his blue uniform, she in jeans and blouse. Behind them, a picture window framed a panorama of blue skies, wispy clouds, and the office buildings of Portland. On one wall, a Norman Rockwell print underscored their mutual view of their profession. It showed a police officer and a little boy perched on adjacent soda fountain stools, beaming at each other in an obvious glow of good will.

Katie had come to her father's office so they could be filmed together for the video *Straight from the Heart,* which is about families with gay children. Now both laughed as Tom told the interviewer that he had "trained Katie to be heterosexual."

"If I had an agenda for my children," he said, "it was for them to be normal heterosexuals. But Katie turned out to be a normal homosexual." He glanced at his daughter and added, "To me, she's just a great person. And I'm pleased to say, as the chief of police, she's a good cop."

Slim and graceful with brown hair and sparkling brown eyes, Katie bears a striking resemblance to her father. But their bond plainly goes beyond external similarities. Candor, warmth, humor, and an air of self-confidence seem also to run in the genes. Their fondness and respect for each other appear boundless.

Katie clearly deserves her father's "good cop" designation. Her air of friendly openness suggests a youthful innocence; but it masks a smooth blend of toughness, compassion, and sureness of manner that elicits respect from her peers and the citizens of her northeast Portland beat.

Her father is widely acknowledged as one of the most effective chiefs in Portland history. He has won dozens of community, regional, and national awards, and gave the city a new look in law enforcement. He "put in place a style of policing that emphasizes conversation and problem-solving in place of handcuffs and revolving jail doors," according to Portland's daily newspaper, the *Oregonian*. When he retired in mid-1993, the *Oregonian* wrote that in just three years Potter had "brought the bureau closer to the citizens than any chief in contemporary times." Bud Clark, the mayor who appointed him, called him "a very effective administrator" who took the bureau on "a huge leap forward."

But in a retirement interview, Potter predicted that he'd be remembered more for some other things: Marching beside Katie in gay pride parades. Testifying before the state legislature in favor of civil rights protections for gays. Stating publicly that "some of the nicest people in this city are gays and lesbians." Whatever his other accomplishments, as he put it then, "I have no doubt that I will be remembered as 'the gay rights chief.'"

During his first campaign for mayor, Clark had vowed to make the city "a more compassionate place." To that end, in rapid succession, he named and fired three police chiefs who proved unable to move the bureau in the direction Clark envisioned. Finally, Clark settled on Potter, largely because of their shared commitment to the citizen-centered concept known as "community policing." Still, Clark admits to some surprise when Potter announced his intent to wage open battle against what he viewed as the most important roots of social dysfunction and crime: racism, sexism, and homophobia.

Potter kept his vow. His hiring and promotion innovations enriched the bureau's gender and ethnic mix. Revised training programs stressed sensitivity to minorities and women. As one reporter wrote of Chief Potter, the message of equality "practically became his mantra."

Few objected to his stressing justice for women and ethnic minorities. But many Portland citizens were dismayed that he also met regularly with gay and lesbian leaders and openly recruited officers from within their community. He kept a rainbow-striped flag, a gift from the gay community, in his office.

Indeed, the crowning symbol of Potter's open management style was probably his annual appearance in full uniform in Portland's gay pride parade. Criticized for marching in uniform, he said he did it to let the gay community know their police chief believed they deserved the rights guaranteed to all citizens.

These actions angered some officers. One, writing in the police union newspaper, berated Potter's pro-gay stance as "gutless" and "cowardly." Potter became a leading demon and target of the state's powerful radical right. But he retained the support of city officials, and his opinions were paramount in the selection of his successor—Charles Moose, Portland's first African American police chief.

In the closing weeks of Tom's tenure, he and Katie appeared together to deliver a thank-you to a P-FLAG regional conference in Portland. The *Oregonian* reported the event with a banner headline spread over a three-column picture of Tom kissing Katie in front of a huge P-FLAG pennant. It was the emotional highlight of the conference, as delegates stood in a prolonged ovation for their favorite father-daughter team. Some years before, when he was captain of the downtown police precinct, Tom had allowed the local chapter to use a large meeting room in precinct headquarters. He had also attended meetings frequently with Katie and a few times with Katie's mother, Ginger. And now the delegates cheered as he told them, "Some officers felt I was tarnishing the badge. I felt I was burnishing it."

Katie told them what many of them already knew: P-FLAG had played an important role in helping her deeply religious mother overcome her misgivings about Katie's homosexuality. Indeed, some of the P-FLAGgers who rose to applaud that day were long-time Potter family friends. They had quietly rooted as the Potter family survived homosexuality, divorce, and political mudslinging to carve its special niche in police and P-FLAG annals.

In 1991, a report on the Potter family by *Oregonian* writer Janet Filips won an in-house award for feature writing and a commendation as the "consummate story of parental acceptance." In it, Filips reported that the only thing Tom found odd about Katie is that she hates fresh tomatoes. And the story quoted a local psychologist, Carol Landesman, as saying, "Something right happened in that family."

Tom and Ginger's backgrounds appear to be at odds with their acceptance of their daughter's lesbianism. Tom was raised a Southern Baptist in Mississippi until he was ten, when his family moved to Portland; later, at the urging of his deeply religious mother, he spent two years in a San Francisco seminary run by Baptists. While there, he met Ginger, then as now devoutly Baptist. After they were married, he left the seminary to work at a variety of jobs before settling into his law enforcement career in 1966.

Katie was the third of their four children, and her two brothers and an older sister were all married by 1993. Tom remembers Katie as "a loving child—very easy to raise." Over dinner at one of the Potters' favorite Italian restaurants in northwest Portland, he laughs as he tells us, "I hate to say this while she's listening, but she was really a sweet little girl." Across the table, Katie grins, then agrees that she had a wonderful childhood. She explains: "Our parents were always there for us. I'm in awe of how fair they managed to be, doling out the same love to all the kids." Katie, in a long-term relationship with fellow police officer Pam Moen and planning to have children of her own, says she hopes *she* can be that kind of parent.

Tom has no doubt as to her potential as a mother. "Her nieces and nephews absolutely love her," he says. "I watch Katie around children and I can't wait until she has her own."

Tom and Ginger are divorced and Ginger is remarried. But the entire family gathers with friends several times a year for holidays. The clan now includes Ginger's second husband, Fred Hall; Tom's companion, Jeanna Cernazanu; the three married Potter children and their families; and Katie and Pam. And, notes Tom, "It's not, 'Here's all these couples and here's Katie and her partner.' It's just,

'Here's our family.'" Indeed, Katie counts older sister Kim among her best friends, and the frequent reunions are happy times for the entire extended family.

It was Katie's affection and respect for her father that first led her, at age five, to think about becoming a cop. But her fondest fantasy—patrolling at her father's side—never came to pass. "I had these dreams about a father-daughter team on the street, in a squad car. I still think it would be neat." But long before Katie reached the academy, her father was moving up in the department and away from the street.

As a child, Katie was passionately devoted to sports, and she eventually won a college softball scholarship. By that time, however, she was being tormented inwardly by unwanted crushes on other girls and women. "I don't *want* to feel this," she told herself.

Meanwhile, alerted primarily by her tomboy nature, her father had begun to consider the possibility Katie might be gay. To him, it was not a daunting prospect. He had long before shaken off the judgmental religious conditioning of his youth. As a schoolboy in Portland, he sat next to black youngsters whose pains and joys seemed no different from his own. Later, he worked with all kinds of people, including some who were gay. The cramped world view of his early church upbringing was transformed into a passion for inclusiveness. So he was not disturbed that Katie might not be a heterosexual.

The first thing to put him on notice, Tom says, was her devotion to jeans. "When they were little," he says, "we would dress Katie and Kim in pretty little dresses for church on Sunday. Kim would want to keep her dress on all day. But Katie would take hers off as soon as we got home and put on jeans."

Katie's path was eased by signals of her father's understanding and tolerance. She remembers an incident when she was fifteen when she, Kim, and Tom were going to pick up napkins for Kim's wedding. Katie froze when the subject suddenly turned to homosexuality and Kim expressed a certain distaste. But she relaxed when her father casually assured Kim that "they're just like every-body else."

Still, it would be another four years before she came out to her father. It happened over tacos at a Mexican restaurant, and Tom says he had guessed what she was planning when Katie invited *him* out: "It made me suspicious, because normally old Dad foots the bill for that." Unsurprised by the news, he assured her he would do everything he could to help her feel comfortable with herself or smooth the way with other family members.

Katie's siblings took the news relatively calmly, but her mother had deep religious qualms. Ginger and Tom had been divorced a few years before ("Our philosophies had become too different for us to live together," says Tom); and Ginger had been bitter for a time. But their mutual stake in the children spurred a renewal of good relations.

So when Tom and Katie suggested that Ginger attend a P-FLAG meeting, she agreed. There, she met other parents who had had to overcome similar religious misgivings, and recovery began.

For Katie, though, the process was too slow. She nearly gave up on her mother after one discouraging incident that occurred in Ginger's office, where her mother kept a picture of a younger Katie with long wavy hair and wearing what Katie calls "this frilly little gown." Ginger looked at her short-haired, jeans-clad daughter, then gazed longingly at the picture and said, "You know, you were so pretty then." Katie, hurt and angry over what she perceived as her mother's insensitivity, vowed not to see Ginger anymore. A talk with her father helped calm her. "He did what he does so well, comforting you but at the same time helping you see the other person's perspective."

Moved by Katie's apparent pain ("She was acting angry, but I knew that was the hurt speaking"), Tom also went to see Ginger. Over a series of lunches, he reminded her of what she had heard at P-FLAG meetings, and gently led her through a re-examination of her personal and religious values.

Ginger says the easy part was recognizing that what had changed was not Katie—she was still the same person—but rather Ginger's own thinking about her daughter. The religion hurdle was more difficult. Ultimately, she came to believe that God created Katie complete with her sexual orientation and "would not condemn what he created." Katie, she concluded, was simply who she was meant to be.

Katie remembers the day, years after she had come out, that the barriers between herself and her mother were finally dissolved. They were driving together to visit Ginger's parents, and for the first time in years, they spoke freely. In Katie's words, "all our dirty laundry got out, and the air was cleared."

Tom plainly takes equal joy in Ginger's change of attitude. While the subject of Katie's gayness still disturbs her, he says, the nature of her distress has changed. Once it was, "Why has this happened to me?" Now it's, "Why are people critical of gays and lesbians?" Ginger no longer just tolerates Katie but loves her unconditionally, Tom says.

Sitting at dinner with Tom and Katie, I am struck by how little they fit the stereotypes of cops. To hear them talk, you might assume they were in social work or some other type of ministry to the needy, oppressed, and mistreated. They both say, for example, that they chose their calling largely out of a desire to help others.

"That's what it's all about—helping other people and feeling good about what you've done at the end of the day," Tom says, poking the air with a spaghetti-wrapped fork for emphasis.

Katie concurs. She recalls an incident the evening before in which she had arrested a young man who had brutally attacked his seventy-one-year-old aunt before a neighbor intervened and the attacker fled. After a high-speed chase, Katie and two other officers captured the man.

But it wasn't the derring-do that was etched in Katie's mind. Instead, it was the greeting she received from the elderly victim—

whom she knew personally from her patrols—when Katie returned to interview her. "When I walked through the door, she gave me a big smile and said, 'Oh, I'm so glad it's you.' I could just see the comfort it brought her that it was me who came through the door and not some unknown in a blue uniform. It made me feel good to be a cop."

One cold February night in 1994, I personally witnessed the mixture of command and compassion she brings to the job, when I rode with Katie for a few hours in Car 631.

On one call, she was questioning witnesses in a crowded bar where a robbery had occurred fifteen minutes earlier. One of the patrons described the culprit as "a nigger shit." Quietly and crisply, Katie commanded, "I don't like that kind of language. Just tell me what happened without any editorials." Daunted, the man cleaned up his language. But he was obviously drunk, and Katie left orders with the bartender to serve him no more drinks.

Back in the squad car, while she was telling me that domestic calls can be the most dangerous of all to an officer, her radio announced an "armed robbery in progress" at a fast-food restaurant. Katie switched on her rooftop lights and quickly accelerated to sixty miles per hour.

As we careened down narrow city streets, she calmly explained that she had her siren off so as not to warn the perpetrator. A few blocks from the restaurant, she turned off the roof lights, too, and then parked the car down a side street a half-block away. She swiftly jumped out, ordering me to wait near the car.

I watched as she moved quickly and stealthily, right hand on holster, toward the restaurant. She disappeared around a corner; and I quickly looked for some spot that would provide a protected view of whatever might ensue. Before I could find one, Katie returned, relaxed. The alarm had been inadvertently tripped by an employee.

Moments later, the radio crackled again, directing Katie to the home of a woman who had reported receiving threatening telephone calls. Now I saw Katie's softer side. As we entered the house, the woman's young daughter peered up at Katie with troubled eyes. "Are you a cop?" she asked. "I sure am, honey," Katie replied, with a smile and a soothing manner. "Are you going to arrest somebody?" the girl asked. Again, the soothing smile framed the answer, "Oh, no. Your mom just wants to talk to me about a problem she's having. I'm here to help her." The little girl now grinned back happily, as at a new friend.

Tom had always told Katie not to be deterred from coming out by concerns for his career. So in early 1991, when a writer for a local gay journal suggested doing a feature story about them, Katie agreed and Tom cooperated fully. As soon as the publication hit the stands, the mainstream media swarmed over the story. A proud and openly gay police officer, openly supported by an equally proud father who was also her chief, added up to a front-page nugget.

Within the bureau, Tom says, Katie took most of the heat. "As chief, you don't have a lot of people in the organization telling you, 'Hey, I think you and your daughter are full of stuff.' But I don't think she realized the firestorm that would come down on *her* head."

Katie had built a network of close friends within the bureau, but others turned hostile. Wild rumors circulated that she was having sex with young girls. Her personal car was vandalized when she parked it in the police parking lot during a gay pride parade. One officer with whom she had been on "joking-around" terms stopped talking to her; others made snide remarks about the gay pride parade in her presence. She was the butt of subtle but pointed insults: the officer handing out car keys and radios to her shift, for example, would sometimes ignore her, forcing her to walk around the counter to gather her own equipment.

The harassment dwindled over the years, but Katie notes in soft tones, "I don't know if I've ever told him, but I don't think I'd still be in the bureau if it wasn't for Dad's support. He gave me the understanding and strength to keep going, assuring me that we did the right thing."

Tom, with the perspective of greater age, sees Katie as a "kind of a lightning rod" for a force that is already beginning to play itself out. In the 1960s, cops had to learn to accept blacks, and then in the 1970s, to accept women. There is just one group that it's still acceptable to hate, to call dirty names, and to discriminate against, and that's gay people. And Potter is optimistic that cops will learn to accept them, too—and become better cops in the process. "In a few years, this won't be the issue it is today," he says.

When pressed, Tom will admit he didn't wholly avoid the ugliness triggered by Katie's coming out. During the 1992 gay pride celebration, for example, a television reporter approached him to check a rumor she had heard at an anti-gay press conference held earlier that day. "She looked at me, mike in hand, cameras rolling, and said, 'The rumor is that you have sex with small boys. Is that true?'" Tom was so startled at the question, all he could do was laugh. Only later, when he thought about the mean-spiritedness behind the rumor, did he become angry.

Similar nastiness followed him down to his final press conference, at which he announced his retirement. He was stepping down, he said, because he felt he had accomplished what he had set out to do, and because he wanted to do new things, such as traveling and getting a degree in archaeology. A reporter asked, "But how is your health?" It was fine, Tom answered, with the possible exception of a little high blood pressure. Later, in private, the reporter told him he had gotten a call from someone in the Police Bureau who said Potter was retiring because he had AIDS.

"Some people are so homophobic," he says, "they can't understand that anyone would support gays and lesbians simply because it's the right thing to do, or because gays and lesbians are decent and caring people entitled to their civil rights. They have to imagine, 'Well, he must be one of those himself.'"

A local psychologist, quoted in the *Oregonian*, marveled at Tom's apparent unconcern about the jeopardy to his own position or the inevitable vilification of him as the father of a lesbian. To Katie, though, that's hardly cause for surprise.

"I see how people might feel he risked everything, and I'm very proud of him," she says. "But to me it's just the way he's always been. He was just being normal."

The Surgeon

Pat Thorne says her youngest child, Tracy, differed from her other two in one notable respect.

"When his brother and sister were little, if somebody spilled something on the floor, and I'd say, 'Who did this?' they'd say, 'Not me.' Tracy was different. He'd say, 'I did.' That's just the way he was.

"He'd always tell you whatever was on his mind. At times, I wished he'd be more tactful."

Tracy was also bright, gregarious, and a natural leader. In high school, he was president of several organizations while lettering in cross country and serving as the manager of the football team. At Vanderbilt University, he was a member of the executive committee of his fraternity for three years, and its president when he was a senior.

Pat's concern about Tracy's frankness resurfaced in the summer of 1988, when an exhilarated Tracy gathered the family together to announce he had decided to join the Navy. "I could see he was really excited about the Navy. But I wondered if he could take orders without telling his superiors whatever he might be thinking," she recalls.

For four years, it appeared as though her worries were groundless. Tracy's Navy career soared.

When he decided to enlist, he was still a senior political science major at Vanderbilt. But a week after graduation, in May 1989, he joined seventy-one other officer candidates at Pensacola Naval Air

Station. Four months later, he was commissioned an ensign, completing officer training with outstanding achievement awards in both academics and physical training.

But greater distinctions were to come, first in flight training and later as a bombardier/navigator in an elite squadron known as the "Flying Tigers." In four separate phases of his flight training, Tracy finished first in his class, winning Top Gun honors as the outstanding student of the year. As a Flying Tiger, he received the highest performance ratings possible. On two occasions, he was selected as one of only two officers to receive special leadership training. He would later be publicly described by a fellow flier as "one of the finest Navy officers I've ever met." And the captain who pinned on his wings said he hoped Tracy would someday command the Navy.

But the stubborn streak of honesty caught up with Tracy in 1992 when, for the first time in his life, he fell in love—with a man.

At 5'9" and 175 pounds, the ruggedly handsome Tracy strikes a macho image that could easily have camouflaged his gayness and protected his career indefinitely. But he could not, as it were, fly under false colors. He loved the Navy, and accepted its word regarding the qualities—honesty, integrity, loyalty to self—it purported to honor in its officers. On May 19, 1992, Lieutenant Thorne sent his commanding officer a letter saying he was about to announce his homosexuality on *Nightline*.

In college, Tracy had been the only fraternity president to attend meetings about improving conditions for minority students. Now he was ready to stand up for fair play for another minority—his own. He had agreed to go on *Nightline*, he wrote his commanding officer, because he had come to "feel strongly that the Navy's current policy toward homosexuals is unfair."

That night, he said essentially the same thing to a national audience. The next day, members of his squadron—including the commanding officer—expressed support for his courage. But higher up the chain of command, the reaction was swift and hostile.

Within two days, Tracy's name was scraped from his A-6 Intruder attack jet; he was detached from his squadron, and discharge proceedings were begun.

On July 23-24, 1992, a three-officer board of review convened at Oceana Naval Air Station in Virginia Beach to consider the case. Some two dozen correspondents jostled in the cramped hearing room to report on what amounted to a fait accompli. Tracy's lawyer offered seventy-nine witnesses and exhibits that were ruled irrelevant and inadmissible. The proffered witnesses included Dr. Lawrence J. Korb, former assistant secretary of defense in the Reagan administration; according to Tracy's lawyer, Korb would have testified that retaining Tracy would not be incompatible with the military mission.

To the board, however, the sole relevant evidence consisted of videotapes from *Nightline*, *The Today Show*, and *CNN Sonya Live* on which Tracy had said he was gay. The Navy had spent some $2 million to train a Top Gun; but under prevailing regulations, his statements on television were deemed sufficient cause to squander superstar talent and substantial taxpayer investment. The board's recommendation to discharge Tracy was foreordained.

But if the three officers were unanimously hostile, Tracy was buoyed by the presence of three civilians who were equally unwavering in their support. They were his parents, Roscoe and Pat, and his sister, Patricia.

The appearance of Roscoe, a West Palm Beach orthopedic surgeon, was a surprise to even the other Thornes. He had objected to Tracy appearing on *Nightline*, and had declined to accompany his wife and daughter when they left home for the hearing. But later, he apparently had a sort of epiphany born of weeks of intensive self-examination. On the second afternoon of the hearing, he strode purposefully into the room and asked to address the panel.

His mere appearance was poignant to his family, and his subsequent impassioned plea to the board provided the dramatic highlight of the hearing. It would spawn articles about him in scores of journals, from the *Miami Herald* to *Harpers* magazine, throughout the country.

In fact, Roscoe came across more as a lumberjack or oil field roustabout than as a physician. Years of pumping iron formed his 235 pounds into mounds of sculptured muscle that rippled over his six-foot frame. Massive shoulders and beefy jowls appeared to meet over the slightest hint of neck. A curly bush of dark brown hair framed a brooding bulldog face that rarely relaxed its scowling intensity.

In 1991, Roscoe dead-lifted 525 pounds in the course of becoming the nation's power-lifting champion for men in his weight class over the age of forty. Roscoe was sixty-one.

He spoke even in ordinary conversation with the same single-minded intensity he brought to pressing iron. He did not suffer fools gladly; and his tone sometimes suggested that the category was reserved primarily for those who differed with his views. He disliked confrontation, and needed to feel ever in control of his surroundings.

So it's not surprising that he was reluctant to talk about the two-month period between learning he had a gay son and his appearance at Tracy's discharge hearing. It was a time when certainty and control must have seemed elusive, a time of dreaded ambivalence, when fixed beliefs clashed with protective parental instincts.

Tracy had come out to his mother and sister in 1991, confident of their support, just months after he had fully acknowledged his homosexuality to himself. But he had delayed telling his father until he was compelled to do so by his decision to go on *Nightline*.

Tracy says his father took the news very badly. He urged Tracy to get a cure through psychiatric treatment, or at least to marry and have children anyway. He adamantly opposed Tracy's planned television appearance. "This doesn't have to leave this room," he pleaded.

While Roscoe shied from discussing his thoughts or feelings during the next months, he plainly was severely distressed. He became uncharacteristically subdued. He refused to watch Tracy on *Nightline.* He sank into an emotional funk that led a colleague to recommend he take a break from his medical practice. He told his family to go to the Virginia Beach hearing without him.

Then, his doubts appear suddenly to have coalesced into powerful conviction. The day before the hearing, Tracy found a message from his father on his answering machine: "I'm coming up. If a father can't stick up for his son, he isn't worth having as a father."

Roscoe hurriedly packed, rushed to the airport, fueled up his private Navajo aircraft, and took off for Virginia Beach. It was only when in the air, he later told Tracy, that he thought about what he wanted to say to the board of review.

In the hearing room, he first listened intently as Tracy made his statement to the panel: "This policy is in complete contradiction to the qualities of a leader the Navy advances. . . . If I cannot be honest with myself, if I cannot respect myself, how can I expect others to respect me?" Looking directly at the three officers, Tracy said, "You are leaders of men. You are not machines. If you allow yourselves to not question a policy that is based on ancient hatred and bigotry and not based on reality, you are allowing yourselves to be machines."

When Tracy finished, Roscoe was granted permission to address the panel. He spoke for nearly half an hour, emotionally and without notes. His first-ever public speech constituted a powerful commentary on the nature and origins of prejudice.

He began quietly, obviously moved by the words he had just heard from his son, recalling Tracy's birth: "A friend of mine took my wife into the delivery room and I waited outside as a young physician. He came out and handed me a baby boy. . . . I put a stethoscope on him, and looked at his arms and his legs, and I thought he was just fine.

"But until I heard this man just now, I didn't realize what a great man was given to me by that doctor friend, delivered to my wife twenty-five years ago."

Then he took the panel to task.

"America, great country that it is, is bleeding because of a lot of wounds, prejudices, that are still left over. . . . And you all are here worrying about a twenty-five-year-old man that has already proved himself beyond a shadow of a doubt as a leader, as a commander, as a superb individual.

"I'm happy to say I'm his father and I wish I could be like him. Forgive me for my emotions, but I wish I could be as good a man as Tracy Thorne is."

Out of his weeks of anguished meditation, Roscoe had concluded that his initial reaction to his son's homosexuality had sprung from his own bias. Now, he reviewed the profound effect of prejudice on his own life.

When he was five, he said, he had a black friend named Jesse. "I was so happy to see him one day, I took him by the hand and I took him up to my white mother, and I said, 'Mama, this is Jesse.' . . . My mother was a real kind, good person and she smiled down at Jesse and she said, 'It's nice to meet you, Jesse.'

"Later that day Jesse went home, and my Mama came over to me and she said, 'Buddy, you never introduce a colored person to a white lady.' I said, 'Yes, Mama, I won't do that anymore.' I was being trained in Jackson, Mississippi by a white woman, my mother, who was a good person, but that's the way she was trained and she was passing it along. She was in the dark. She was living in the darkness, with prejudice, and she was passing that education of darkness on to me."

Later, he said, he saw water fountains and rest rooms marked "colored" and "white." When he was fourteen, he visited California with his parents and saw a restaurant sign that said, "No Mexicans or colored allowed." "That sounded about right to me," he said. "That's the way I'd been trained. I wasn't a Mexican, I wasn't colored, and I went on in.

"I'm responding as I had been trained in the deep South of Jackson, Mississippi. I wasn't thinking for myself."

He remembered his mother taking him to a swimming pool on a trip to Illinois, where a "Gentiles only" sign hung over the gate. "I said, 'Mama, what is a gentile?' And she said, 'Shut up. You're one.' And I went on in. I didn't know what a gentile was, but I was one of them. So I'm being educated all along."

Later, after serving with the infantry in the Korean War, he enrolled at the University of Mississippi. He said there was only one black man on campus, a blind man who sold pencils in front of the administration building. "Everyone loved 'blind Jim.' He wasn't a threat to anybody. So it didn't make any difference that he was on campus or not, because he didn't threaten anybody."

Then he recalled a memory that plainly still pained him. He was working as a graduate pharmacist in a Jackson drugstore, and a young nurse sat down at the soda fountain.

"She had on a pretty white uniform, and she was a registered nurse, but she was a black person. And my boss nudged me in the ribs and said, 'Roscoe, go over there and run her off.'

"I was twenty-five years old, Tracy's age. And I was intelligent, but I had been trained. And so I went over there, and I said, 'You're going to have to leave. We don't want you in here.' And this young nurse looked at me. She was about my age or maybe a little younger, and she was a registered nurse and a fine-looking human being, and tears ran down her cheeks and she left. And I felt so bad.

"I wonder where she is right now, because she's probably about my age. I know she'd remember. I chased her out of the drugstore."

Later, he said, in medical school, his colleagues included a few light-skinned blacks, but "no real black blacks." He noticed, though, that when bodies were dissected in anatomy class, "they all looked pretty much the same." Still later, the government decreed an end to segregation in hospitals. Although he thought it wouldn't work, "We put them together and we treated them. And things were better for it."

In an emotional peroration, he warned the panel members that ruling against Tracy could haunt their consciences: "I want you officers here to know that if you allow anything to happen that would interfere with this young man's ability to have his freedom to serve his country as he so ably proved his ability to do . . . then when you go home tonight, I want each of you to find a good friend. I want you to sit down with that good friend, and I want you to tell him what you allowed to happen."

In the hallway after the hearing, both in tears, Roscoe and Tracy embraced.

"We've got to stop this pain, son," said Roscoe.

Eighteen months later, Roscoe still refused to talk about the weeks that followed Tracy's coming out. Queried directly about that painful time, he told a newspaper reporter he wouldn't have agreed to an interview if he had known he would be asked to "elaborate on me." He would say only, "Any change causes adjustments. . . . And sixty-year-old men don't like to make adjustments, but we have to sometimes, and we're willing to."

In December 1993, I visited Roscoe and Pat in their comfortable West Palm Beach home. I asked Roscoe what had gone on in his mind during that time directly before the hearing; but he would only say that he thought the decision "was instinctive rather than anything else." Parents "always come to the defense of their children, especially if they've been falsely accused or deprived of their rights. That was an instinctive act."

Perhaps, I thought, he simply was reluctant to admit to ever having had feelings that in hindsight seemed to him to be wrong.

Or perhaps, like so many other Americans, he was not yet wholly comfortable with the notion of homosexuality itself.

And, indeed, his attitude in this regard posed something of an anomaly. The man who spoke so eloquently on behalf of his gay son, it turned out, was uneasy with the movement for gay civil rights. At first, he hesitated even to talk to me because he resented the name of my organization, to which I was clearly devoted. Although Pat had had some involvement with P-FLAG, Roscoe had resisted. "I don't like your using the term 'gays and lesbians,'" he said. It is simply wrong, he said, his voice rising, to describe a human being by some single characteristic such as sexual orientation. "You might as well say this man with ingrown toenails, let's put him over here in this category. And, you know, there are some peculiar ones that I'm really watching, and that's those left-handed ingrates. They are a group, and it's time we get some laws passed."

He paused, then spluttered, "Ignorance! We're all just human beings, that's all."

Ironically, the son he so admired was an active spokesman for a movement he apparently resented. And it's a movement, of course, with the ultimate aim of putting itself out of business by making homosexuality a no more significant personal characteristic than ingrown toenails or left-handedness.

During the intense national debate over gays in the military in 1993, Tracy had become a national leader in the campaign for a policy of integration. His classic Norman Rockwell, all-American charisma automatically cast him as a natural spokesman for the cause; he appeared on numerous leading talk shows and before various Congressional committees. He debated admirals and senators and others, coolly and articulately stating the case for equality in the armed services.

At one point, he had a one-on-one meeting with a senator who asked him, "Why can't you keep your private life private?" As Tracy recalls it: "I said, 'Sir, you can't keep your private life private.

Nobody does. You're wearing a wedding ring on your hand, and you have a picture of your wife behind your desk here, and don't tell me you've never cared for somebody so much or had such a great weekend with someone that you came into the office here and talked about them on Monday. Nobody keeps their private life private. What you're asking me to do is consistently, consciously lie, not just not put the picture on my desk, but to consciously and consistently lie to you about who I care about and who I choose to spend my life with. That's what you're asking me to do."

Tracy is clearly of two minds about the frequency with which he is described as an "all-American boy." He knows that image is a powerful asset to him as a spokesman. On the other hand: "A Navy admiral I debated once told me, 'You're okay, you can serve your country, but not these others.' Well, I'm tired of this, because I don't think we should set standards that say gay people have to be all-American in order to serve their country. I just consider myself an everyday, ordinary American who wants to serve his country."

To his parents, of course, he is much more than that. His mother, reconciled to the honesty that ended his stint with the Flying Tigers, feels Tracy "has made a difference—he hasn't just thrown his career away."

Her deepest regret is that her son had to go through a period of torment, alone, before coming to terms with his sexual orientation—and that some of his anguish stemmed from fear that his parents would be hurt.

"We *do* hurt, but because of him hurting," she says. "We don't hurt because he's gay."

Tracy continues to fight his discharge, as challenges to 1993 legislation governing gays in the military—the so-called "don't ask, don't tell" policy—wend a slow path toward the Supreme Court.

On July 11, 1994, Tracy's discharge was up for another hearing, this time in Fort Meyer, Virginia. Roscoe planned once again to speak on behalf of his son, but ten days earlier, he volunteered to fly a friend from West Palm Beach to Orlando. Shortly after takeoff, the Navajo crashed, and Roscoe and his passenger were killed.

As his funeral service began, a biplane circled overhead, streaming a banner with a message from his family: "Roscoe, we love you. We'll miss you."

9

♦

Ministry of Light

Changing Attitudes in Established Religion

Richard Mohr, in *A More Perfect Union*, describes society's treatment of gays as "a grand scale rationalization, a moral sleight-of-hand." His apt point is that anti-gay stereotypes "have a life beyond facts"—that they are mere cover-up for a deeply rooted, irrational cultural prejudice.

This grand-scale rationalizing is nowhere more apparent—or comes with more political and social clout—than in organized religion's traditional enmity toward homosexuality. It is easy to dismiss extremists such as Pat Robertson and Jerry Falwell as massively misguided or mere exploiters of the unsophisticated. But representatives of the conservative arms of the more middle-of-the-road denominations—Catholic, Protestant, and Jewish alike—employ much the same rationalizations. And their arguments serve, however illogically, as the supposed moral underpinning of society's pervasive anti-gay rhetoric.

They proudly proclaim that they act in the name of a loving God, but they strive to preserve the cruel oppression of a class of their fellow citizens. They purport to uphold "family values," but support attitudes that turn parents against children and encourage deceit and fear. They decry promiscuity among gays, but pay little attention to similar behavior among heterosexuals, while denying gay couples the formality of the non-gay world's most effective inducement to monogamy—legal sanction of their unions.

They justify the harassment of perhaps 10 percent of God's creatures by a cramped, selective reading of six or seven ambiguous Bible verses. (See Chapter 5.) But they raise no similar cries about passages that endorse such matters as slavery, incest, and denigration of women, and still others that command unswerving allegiance to dietary and marital laws now universally considered archaic. An example is the story of Lot, which is regularly cited in anti-gay bombast (although incorrectly in the view of many Biblical scholars) as condemning homosexuality. Yet the same text tacitly endorses Lot's offering of his two virgin daughters to satisfy a mob's sexual lusts; and it seems to sanction incest as a means of impregnating daughters whose father is the only available male. Elsewhere in both Old and New Testaments are passages that explicitly approve of slavery—although Paul does direct masters to treat slaves kindly! And throughout the Bible, women are hardly even treated as human beings. The commandment against adultery, for example, is really a law of property; adultery was defined as sex with a married woman, and the sin in question was violating another man's chattel.

Perhaps most paradoxically of all, churches have shunned a cause that in its most basic respects is genuinely spiritual. For the gay movement arises out of millions of individual decisions that acceptance of their God-given natures is part of a quest for wholeness, for actualization of their highest potential.

A few relatively small denominations have acknowledged this commonality between their institutional aims and those of the gay movement. Ordination of openly gay and lesbian ministers or rabbis has been approved by the United Church of Christ, the Unitarian-Universalist Association, and Reform Judaism. For the most part, however, mainline nonfundamentalist churches have been torn for decades by conflict between their conservative and

progressive factions over these issues. Proposals to soften their tra-
ditionally negative positions have been introduced with regulari-
ty. But the measures track a discouragingly predictable path.

Typically, some gay-friendly action will be overwhelmingly
endorsed by a committee of church leaders assigned to study the
issue. Presbyterian, Episcopalian, and Lutheran study groups, by
wide margins, have all urged ordination of openly gay ministers. A
United Methodist committee, by a vote of seventeen to four, recommended revocation of the church's formal declaration that
homosexuality is "incompatible with Christian teachings."

Almost all of these proposals, however, have triggered widespread consternation among the faithful and have been rejected by
the denominational bodies as a whole by lopsided votes. The
Methodist General Conference, for example, rejected by a three-to-
one margin the study committee's recommendation to strike the
"incompatible with Christian teachings" language.

This common pattern demonstrates a couple of truths. The
study groups' overwhelmingly gay-friendly recommendations
plainly indicate that it is almost impossible for those who look
closely at the actual facts to support their churches' traditional
negativism. But just as plainly, most rank-and-file churchgoers are
unwilling to undertake that necessary step of self-education.

In all of these denominations, P-FLAG members are among
those working to make their churches more open and accepting
places. P-FLAG's ranks include numerous ministers, priests, and
rabbis. Seven clergymen, including four bishops, are among its
honorary directors. To these P-FLAG legions, the connections
among religion, spirituality, and gay civil rights are plain.

Consider the experiences of four families.

Carol and Ron Blakley

The Blakleys of Caldwell, Idaho, are one of countless families
throughout the country who are actively encouraging their

churches to live up to their own ideals of love and tolerance. But because their denomination is a relatively small one, their personal impact is perhaps more direct and apparent than that of most of their P-FLAG counterparts in larger churches.

In 1992, Carol was honored by the Boise *Idaho-Statesman* as one of her region's "distinguished citizens." She organized her county mental health association and served on its board for twenty years, performed in local musical and theater productions, presided over a two-state region of the Christian Women's Fellowship, promoted the College of Idaho Fine Arts Series, organized a local community concert series and did counseling at junior high and high school summer conferences. She also sat on her church's highest national administrative body, cared for AIDS hospice patients, chaired her county's first Art Auction and Ball, supported the gay community's Metropolitan Community Church in Boise, held leadership positions with the Girl Scouts and UNICEF, and chaired local political campaigns.

Meanwhile, she somehow found time to raise four children and work as business manager for her husband Ron's company, Blakley Engineers, until their retirement in 1988.

One of the Blakleys' four children, Ronee, is a successful actress. In 1976, she was nominated for an Oscar as best supporting actress for her performance in *Nashville* (for which she also wrote several songs). But much of the drama in the lives of Carol and Ron has arisen from the more prosaic fact that another of their children, Stephen, is gay. That set their deep spirituality on a collision course with organized religion's pervasive hostility to homosexuality.

Carol and Ron belong to the Christian Church (Disciples of Christ), an indigenous North American denomination of approximately a million souls in the United States and Canada. Carol has been active at all levels of church affairs, and served on the denomination's General Board from 1973 to 1981.

In rural Idaho, open proponents of gay rights were probably

rarer than citrus trees when Steve, then twenty-one, came out to his parents in a moving letter in 1972. So while Carol and Ron fully supported Steve, they considered his sexual orientation strictly a family matter for some years. Then, in late 1976, one of the church's top officials visited Caldwell, and Carol determined to take advantage of his presence. She showed him Steve's letter; and before he left Caldwell, she had enlisted his support for a proposal to ordain openly gay ministers. As a result, a recommendation to that effect was endorsed by the 480-member General Board and presented to the church's 1977 General Assembly in Kansas City.

There, it met the usual fate of such measures: The church body as a whole rejected it. Not satisfied, anti-gay forces at the convention proposed a resolution condemning "the homosexual lifestyle." In response, Carol rose on the floor, clutching Steve's five-year-old letter. Shakily at first, but with increasing confidence and passion, she read it to her fellow delegates.

His revelation began by addressing several myths: "I am a homosexual. I am not sick, nor deviate, nor mentally ill. My sexuality simply expresses itself in attraction for other men rather than women. Neither is it unnatural. I am not attracted to children, nor pain nor heterosexual men. For me it is completely natural and right and good."

> If your morality would condemn me, first consider these things: I did not choose to be homosexual, but I found myself one and have accepted it, happily, as an integral part of my personality; the morality that could condemn me for something over which I have no control must itself be without humaneness, akin to the consciousness which gassed Jews and massacred Indians; homosexuals in this country and others have for centuries been forced to lead secretive lives, in constant fear that their careers would be destroyed and the relationships with their loved ones cut off by hate and disgust.

I refuse to hate myself and I refuse to allow anyone who wishes to have continued personal contact with me to hate this essential part of my self either. I also refuse to live in the half-world of
gay ghettoes, where furtive sexual liaisons pass for love and self-
revulsion and secretiveness are the prevailing mode.

I do not live a life surrounded only by gay men. All my
friends, both in Idaho and here, have for a long time accepted this
facet of my personality without reservation, knowing that I was
a whole being divisible into acceptable and unacceptable parts.
My two beautiful sisters have shown me only warmth and love
and remarkable understanding, as I hope my brother will when
he is old enough to comprehend the implications of the oppressive social stigma attached to my sexuality. I will not live a life of
fear and shame. Too many important matters interest me for me
to spend my life concerned with other peoples' unjust and inhu-
mane moral prejudices.

It is very important that you, as parents, not feel guilty because
I, your son, am a homosexual. Guilt implies fault and fault implies
a misdeed, and I cannot consider myself as some mistake, to be
altered if at all possible and accepted only with resignation. I must
ask you to accept me fully, as a human being worthy of respect
and trust and love. I am no less than any other being simply
because I am a homosexual!

Finally, I hope that you can accept this part of me without
reservations and regrets. . . . I believe that your capacity to love
can encompass the totality of myself and that you will know that
I am the very same son that you have known for twenty-one
years. If I disappoint you, I am sorry, but I cannot spend my life
in apology. I must look to the future and so must you. . . .

As Carol, "choked up and teary," finished reading, thousands
of delegates rose in a rousing ovation that doomed the anti-gay
resolution. And Carol herself was launched on a career of church
leadership that would include three years of service on the

denomination's top policy-making body, the Administrative Committee of the General Board.

"I have never felt such power," Carol says of the ovation she received that day. "I believe the Lord was there. He opened the door and dared me step through it." But she adds, as though embarrassed by this implicit admission of the depth of her spiritual feelings, "Of course I know there are those who would say it was the devil who opened the door."

Carol received waves of requests for copies of Steve's letter, and she has distributed hundreds of copies of it over the years. Meanwhile, back home, the Boise *Idaho-Statesman* got wind of what had happened in Kansas City and picked up the story. A banner headline blared, "Caldwell Family Stands by Homosexual Son." The article blew the family out of the closet.

These events led to a deeper involvement with P-FLAG and the gay community in Boise, and local gay groups have since honored both Carol and Ron with service awards. Within their church, Carol's dramatic 1977 convention appearance was the catalyst for the formation of an organization called Gay and Lesbian Affirming Disciples (GLAD). In 1985, Carol was honored with the first GLAD award, and eight years later, the annual prize was named after her. The Christian Church has become somewhat warmer to its gay and lesbian worshipers, and a few of its thirty-six regions now grant individual congregations the discretion to hire openly gay ministers.

Steve Blakley, who runs a Los Angeles copy-writing firm, says wryly of his parents' activism that they are "in a way, eccentric." He explains: "They truly believe that people are good and that if you are good, others will respond in kind."

Bishop Mel Wheatley

I feel a sort of awe when I contemplate the devotion of gay and lesbian worshipers. I find myself taking special note in gay newspapers of the many advertisements of gay religious groups. (Mostly, they bear such inspirational names as the Catholics' "Dignity," the Methodists' "Affirmation," and the Episcopalians' "Integrity"; but I also discovered a Jewish group known as "Chutzpah.") I even found myself moved, at a gay pride parade, by a seemingly silly chant of a group of marching Latter Day Saints: "Two, four, six, eight, all Mormons are not straight."

In part, I am responding to the poignant example of persons whose faith is so important to them that they refuse to abandon the churches that have abandoned them. But I am also responding to my increasing awareness that the coming-out process contains a spiritual element—that it is a quest for what religionists sometimes call "the authentic self."

I also sense that my own P-FLAG experience has spiritual meaning. Having a gay child pits the instinct of parental love against entrenched social norms. To resolve the conflict, family members need to find answers to questions about human values and the meaning of personal integrity. At P-FLAG, we undertake the search with a community of fellow seekers motivated by the same pressing concerns. It's a process with wonderful rewards, not the least of which is an expanding appreciation of the richness of human diversity.

To me, such a process by definition must have a spiritual element. However, I kept the thought to myself for a long time, for I felt it was inappropriate to suggest that spirituality could have any bearing on dealing with a child's sexuality. Then I heard a Methodist bishop say essentially the same thing.

The bishop, Melvin Wheatley, Jr., also says that he and his wife now find more spiritual renewal in a P-FLAG meeting than they do in church. P-FLAG, he says, is their "primary nurture and support group," one that renews them for their professional, religious, and community leadership roles.

Wheatley is one of the bishops on P-FLAG's slate of honorary directors. Until his retirement in 1984 at age seventy, he was bishop of the four-state Denver Area of the United Methodist Church. During his distinguished career, he received many kudos, including honorary degrees from two major universities and designations as Stockton, California's "Young Man of the Year," the Los Angeles Church Federation's "Clergyman of the Year," and American University's "Alumnus of the Year."

He and his wife Lucile were pioneers in the movements against racism and sexism. In the 1940s, they even moved into the home of a Japanese-American family in the hope that their presence would shield the family from being taken to a relocation camp. (It didn't.) And in the 1970s, Wheatley became the nation's first clergyman of distinction to speak out forcibly against organized religion's general condemnation of gay people.

His opposition to anti-gay church pronouncements and policies put him in the national spotlight. In a 1982 *New Yorker* article, Calvin Trillin described an effort within Methodism to have the church view homosexuals "not as wretched sinners, but as . . . individuals of sacred worth . . . who can be Christians without qualification." Trillin reported that the effort "sometimes seemed like a one-man crusade." The one man was Wheatley.

Even as Trillin wrote, a counter-crusade was forming. Later that same year, Wheatley was in the news again when another minister and eighty-eight parishioners lodged formal charges of heresy against him. Their complaint: Wheatley had made pro-gay statements and named an openly gay minister to a Denver church.

If those strike the reader as less than stake-burning crimes, a subsequent committee of investigation was of similar mind. The panel not only found no basis for the charges, but acknowledged the need within the church for "continuing study, reflection, and debate" on homosexuality. Wheatley, it said, "has addressed this concern in the light of Scripture, tradition, reason, and experience in keeping with the pursuit of truth characteristic of our United Methodist heritage."

The Associated Press wire-story about the event included a

photograph of Wheatley receiving a congratulatory hug from his son Paul in the Los Angeles church where the hearing and ruling had taken place. Another son, Jim, a lawyer, had helped present his father's case before the panel. But a third son, John, had the largest personal stake in the case. He had been his father's principal source of revelation, and most immediate motivational force, for that one-man crusade. He was gay.

It had been more than a decade since John had come out to his parents. But, Mel says, "Lucile and I never went through the agony that most P-FLAG parents went through. We knew immediately that if John was gay, the stereotypes must be false." They also knew, he says, "We wouldn't feel comfortable being anywhere John wouldn't be welcome."

The seeds of Wheatley's break with denominational orthodoxy were sown in 1978, when he and Lucile hosted a Colorado meeting of the United Methodist Council of Bishops. The agenda included a motion that the Council reaffirm its support for a statement on homosexuality in the church's governing law. The statement was clear and damning: "[W]e do not condone the practice of homosexuality and consider it incompatible with Christian teaching."

Wheatley alone objected. In addition to their son John, he and Lucile had long had a number of cherished friends who were gay. To the Wheatleys, as Mel told the other bishops, the church law statement was a "pronouncement on real people, not a pronouncement on a subject without a face." So he felt compelled to violate "the protocol calling for quiescent agreeableness on the part of hosts."

Mel calls this his personal coming-out statement. He told the others that he and Lucile had found their lives "incredibly enriched by gays who were living fulfilled and fulfilling lives." He described four of them in particular, including their son John and a lifelong friend, a doctor, whom Wheatley credited with having saved his life twenty-three years earlier. "The total life of each one of the four," he said, "appears to me and to Lucile to be as close to authentic Christian living as we perceive ourselves to be."

More pointedly—"out of my own sense of integrity"—Wheatley issued an ultimatum. Any public declaration of the council's pronouncement reaffirming the negative language, he insisted, must "carry the unmistakable message that the vote that launched it was not unanimous." In subsequent months, he reiterated his position to the other bishops in letters and calls.

His colleagues ignored the warning. Perhaps, misled by Wheatley's collegial and congenial manner, they underestimated his resolve. The 1980 General Conference quadrennial "state of the church" report endorsed the anti-gay statement without a disclaimer of unanimity; and Wheatley went public, causing an intradenominational fissure that remains agape to this day. Newspaper accounts of his dissent reveal that he wore the button of Affirmation, the Methodist gay group, throughout the 1980 convention. His stance evoked hundreds of letters, pro and con. But this was only a trickle compared to the gusher of mail that greeted the next Wheatley foray into controversy.

Until the Reverend Julian Rush was in his mid-forties, he once said, he "lived out the white-picket-fence blueprint." He was married, father of two children, and a popular minister of education at the First United Methodist Church of Boulder, Colorado. Then, after a divorce, he acknowledged to himself what he had denied all his life: he was gay.

He also acknowledged it to a few others at First Church, and that set off the chain of events that resulted in the heresy charges against Mel Wheatley. Despite Rush's immense popularity among the youth, and among the parents and others who knew him through his gifted work with the young people, he lost his post in 1981. The church was badly split on the issue. But in the end, as one member put it during a congregational meeting, the decision was governed by the golden rule: "Those who have the gold make the rules." And at First Church, that meant primarily the older, more conservative members of the congregation.

As Rush's bishop during the dispute, Wheatley supported his retention. And after Rush was ousted, Wheatley assigned him as a part-time minister at a Denver church.

In a pastoral letter to the clergy of the Rocky Mountain Conference in November 1981, Wheatley defended his appointment of an openly gay minister both as a matter of church law and of morality. The first two pages of the letter contained a tightly reasoned analysis of the technical legitimacy of his move. But more noteworthy was the third page, which contained some personal perspectives that Wheatley told the clergy "may help you further understand my official response." They form a passage that is regularly cited and circulated by both religious and lay groups. It is part of the packet received by all parents who ask for literature from the national P-FLAG office. It is perhaps unsurpassed in its lyric articulation of both the logic and the soul of the pro-gay— indeed, pro-human—message.

The passage responds to the question, "Do I believe that homosexuality is a sin?"

> I am an enthusiastically heterosexual male. Is my heterosexuality a virtue, a sign of righteousness, an accomplishment or victory of some kind on my part? Of course not. I had nothing whatsoever to do with my *being* heterosexual. My sexual orientation is a mysterious gift of God's grace, communicated through an exceedingly complex set of chemical, biological, chromosomal, hormonal, environmental, developmental factors totally outside my control. My heterosexuality is a gift—neither a virtue nor a sin. What I *do* with my heterosexuality, however, *is* my personal, moral, and spiritual responsibility. My behavior as a heterosexual may be sinful—brutal, exploitive, selfish, promiscuous, superficial. My behavior as a heterosexual, on the other hand, may be beautiful—tender, considerate, loyal, other-centered, profound.

Precisely the same distinction between *being* homosexual and *behaving* as a homosexual applies as to heterosexuals. Homosexuality, quite like heterosexuality, is neither a virtue nor an accomplishment. Homosexual orientation is a mysterious gift of God's grace communicated through an exceedingly complex set of chemical, biological, chromosomal, hormonal, environmental, developmental factors totally outside my homosexual friends' control. Their homosexuality is a gift, neither a virtue nor a sin. What they do with their homosexuality, however, is definitely their personal, moral, and spiritual responsibility. Their *behavior* as homosexuals may be very sinful—brutal, exploitive, selfish, promiscuous, superficial. Their behavior as homosexuals, on the other hand, may be beautiful—tender, considerate, loyal, other-centered, profound.

With this interpretation of the mystery that must be attributed to both heterosexual and homosexual orientations, I clearly do not believe that homosexuality is a sin.

Others, of course, did so believe. By now, with his pro-gay statements and his appointment of Rush to the Denver church, Wheatley had aroused the denomination's right wing. The heaviest fire came from an unofficial fundamentalist church caucus known as Good News. A group of its ministers attacked Wheatley's pro-gay views generally, and said the Rush appointment in particular would "undermine the basic foundation for our faith and Christian ethic—the Holy Scriptures." Within weeks, that sentiment sparked the heresy charges from which Wheatley was ultimately cleared.

Despite his unequivocal exoneration, Wheatley continued to draw fire from bands of diehard fundamentalists. Good News went on inciting letters of protest. One Colorado church filed a formal request that Wheatley be "involuntarily retired." Other congregations passed votes of censure; and at least ten showed their displeasure by reducing or eliminating their contributions to the Rocky Mountain Conference.

But plaudits also flowed. As the first high churchman to openly defend gays' equality before God, Wheatley found himself with
some important interdenominational support. A national "Friends
of Bishop Wheatley" committee was formed, largely to collect
money to replace the withheld congregational contributions, and
the effort attracted national figures. One of the nation's leading theologians, Harvard Divinity Professor Harvey Cox, a Baptist, said he
"signed on gladly" because he believed in Wheatley's stance. R.
Marvin Stuart, Wheatley's predecessor as the Methodists' Denver-
area bishop, called Wheatley "exceedingly courageous" and "the
essence of integrity and compassion." Other members included
Right Reverend Paul Moore, Episcopal bishop of New York, and
Dottie Lamm, wife of then-Colorado governor Richard Lamm.

Among the staunchest of Wheatley's supporters was the
Denver chapter of P-FLAG, then known as Parents and Friends of
Gays. After Wheatley was "acquitted" of heresy, the chapter took a
quarter-page advertisement in the *Denver Post* "to say a public
'Thank You'" for his support of gays. Recalling that event, Wheatley
says he and Lucile "agreed at the time that we should be putting an
ad in the paper thanking P-FLAG for *its* support." And he adds:
"We are continuing to try to live out our appreciation."

The Wheatleys had been introduced to P-FLAG in 1978, eight
years after John had told them he was gay. Through John, they
had met numbers of gay men they liked and admired, in particular John's partner, Jim Babl. They knew about the Denver group
and had been urged by friends to attend meetings, but never had.
Then one day Lucile took some food to a close friend, Elinor
Lewallen, who was recovering from cancer surgery.

Elinor seemed depressed and Lucile asked if something was
troubling her. In tears, Elinor said she had just learned she had a
lesbian daughter. Lucile recalls, "I told her, 'I might understand better than you think, because we have a gay son.' That just blew her
away."

So Lucile offered to accompany Elinor to a support meeting,

and they went. Impressed, Lucile urged Mel to attend a subsequent meeting with her. The rest, as they say, is important P-FLAG history: not only did the Wheatleys form their own rich relationship with the organization, but nine years later, Lewallen became P-FLAG's second national president. Moreover, Elinor's husband, Tom, served several years, ending in 1992, as regional director for P-FLAG's Mountain district.

Mel Wheatley refers to P-FLAG meetings as "rap groups." For him, the secret of their dynamic is contained in Martin Buber's theological classic, I and Thou.

The heart of the Buber theology is what he termed the "I-Thou" concept. Social problems arise, he said, when one person relates to another not as a person, an entity sacred in the sight of God (a "Thou"), but as a thing (an "It"), a vehicle for the accomplishment of some selfish end. Most human relationships are "I-It" affairs. But when there is a true meeting of two persons, of "I" and "Thou," the spirit of creativity, of life-enhancement, is present.

As Mel explains, "In so many of the meetings we all participate in, there is no true 'meeting' of the people who are there. Everybody speaks in a guarded way, with a low element of risk, which means a low element of trust." In other words, people are engaging in "I-It" dialogue. But not so, Wheatley says, at the rap groups. "After participating in P-FLAG for a while, it began to dawn on us that we were never in a meeting where people didn't risk saying more about themselves than they ever had before."

He points out that when people at P-FLAG meetings talk about the feelings engendered by knowing they have a gay child—it may merely be the sentence, "I have a gay child"—they often are saying the words for the first time. That's trust—revealing a never-before-disclosed aspect of the real you. It means you are trusting others to respond in kind and to treat your disclosure with care and consideration. At P-FLAG they usually do just that. In part it happens because trust begets trust. But it also happens because at least some of the others have experienced what you're going through, and still others have parents who have or soon will be. So your words are almost certain to touch others in some meaningful place of their own. As Wheatley puts it: "Everyone there is at a degree of risk and is participating on the basis of trust. It's the 'I-Thou' factor at work. It produces a level of energy, of love and friendship, that reaches dimensions other groups just don't reach."

Although the Wheatleys' son John died of melanoma cancer in 1984, the same year Mel retired, the couple are surrogate parents for scores of young lesbians and gay men who meet them at P-FLAG; and they have retained warm ties with Jim Babl and other longtime gay and lesbian friends. In 1990, they were among eight P-FLAG members who sang with the Festival Chorus at the first Gay Games in Vancouver, British Columbia. They rarely miss a major gay pride parade; a picture of them among the estimated 750,000 participants in a 1993 gay rights march on Washington graced the pages of the national Methodist newsletter that year.

At the first P-FLAG convention Myrna and I attended, in Chicago, Wheatley conducted a nondenominational worship service. His comments that Sunday included a sentiment that at the time struck me as somewhat fanciful, but which I would learn is shared by thousands of P-FLAG parents. It is the notion that having a gay child not only need not dim one's life, but can actually enhance it—the apparent tragedy can mask a golden opportunity to grow in understanding and appreciation of others.

"We were not wise enough to pray for gay children," Wheatley said. "But now we are smart enough to thank God for sending those gay children to us."

Jane Spahr

P-FLAG's ranks include numerous couples whose marriages ended, but whose friendships did not, when one of the partners turned out to be gay. After the inevitable anguish of readjustment, love and affection *can* survive. The revelation irretrievably transforms the nature of a relationship; but the relationship itself often revives and flourishes.

The experiences of these couples reveal the regenerative power of personal integrity, truth-telling, and respect for individual differences. They demonstrate that sexual orientation is an important but not defining aspect of personal identity. And they can speak to the spiritual dimension of the coming-out process and, indeed, of sexuality itself.

One such story, a staple of P-FLAG lore, is that of Jane and Jim Spahr. In 1991, Jane, who had been ordained seventeen years earlier, made ecclesiastical history as the first openly gay minister to be called as a pastor of a Presbyterian church. She was ultimately denied the post by order of the denomination's highest judicial commission; and her case rocked the national church body, reflecting a deep schism in the denominational soul. Through it all, she retained Jim's staunch support, although they had been divorced for nearly fifteen years.

When Jim and Jane were married in 1964, they added a phrase to their vows stating that each would love the other "from now until eternity." Jim has remarried, and Jane has since been in a long-term relationship with another woman cleric, Coni Staff. But that 1964 vow is as strong as ever.

Jim and Jane are in frequent touch with other couples torn by the revelation that one of them is gay. Jim tells them, "Janie and I just got new information, but we're keeping our vows. We will love one another forever."

So when Jim and his wife Jackie decided in 1992 to hold a recommitment ceremony for their tenth anniversary, it was only natural for them to ask Jane to officiate. After all, she was the minister who had conducted their first wedding ceremony! Jim and Jackie also asked that Coni assist in the recommitment rites.

The event was held in a rose garden in Petaluma, California, and was attended by some fifty friends and family members, including Jim and Jane's two sons, Chet and Jimmy, and Jackie's daughter, Wanda. "We all cried," Jane says. "The ceremony was touching, just beautiful. It was so good to have our whole family there together."

In an unusual twist even for such an unusual tale, it was Jim who first considered the possibility that Jane was a lesbian. Almost from the beginning of their marriage, he sensed "something in Janie's life that wasn't up front every day." He silently resolved to support her, whatever might come. Jim says he was only being selfish—that if the marriage were to end, he wanted to maintain sufficient harmony to protect his own relationship with their still very young sons. But whatever his motivation, the result has been the creation of a warm and close extended family.

Jane's personal recognition of her gayness came one day in the mid-1970s at a conference addressed by two gay ministers, one male and one female. As she listened, she thought, "My God. This is *my* story." She went home, burst into the house, and said, "Jim, I've got to say this out loud: I'm a lesbian." He said, "I know. I've been waiting for you to tell me."

At the time, Jimmy was nine and Chet was seven. Their parents had already talked to them about sex some two years earlier. They had never heard about homosexuality; so when told Jane was attracted to other women, they simply accepted it without judgment. ("Because our parents were open from the start, it was much easier for us to deal with," says Jimmy, now twenty-eight.) Their father told them that people would say their parents were breaking up because their mother was a lesbian; but it was just as true, he said, that they were doing so because he was heterosexual and couldn't meet her needs, either.

Jane was then an assistant minister at a Presbyterian church in San Rafael, just south of Petaluma. Ironically, one of her close friends there was Jackie, who had not yet even met Jim. Over the years, the women's friendship has deepened.

Jim and Jackie frequently join Jane and Coni to form a speaking team at colleges and community groups. As a foursome, they've also counseled numerous couples who are forced to split because one or the other is gay. So Jane, Jim, and Jackie are not your typical lovers' triangle. Listen to them.

Jane: "People say things like, 'If only she had the right man.' Well, I *had* the right man. And Jackie is a very special person. It's a relief and joy that Jim has found someone who is right for him."

Jim: "I spent fourteen years living with Janie Spahr. I know who she is, and I know I'm damned proud to have been her partner. And I'm always the father of her children. That's quite an honor."

Jackie: "I'm sometimes asked whether I don't find the situation a little strange. I say, 'Well, Janie was my pastor long before I knew Jim, Janie and I are wonderful friends, and yes, I married Jim, and we're all doing just fine, thanks.'"

Jane's preaching style has been described as warm, witty, outspoken, and stimulating. She walks around the sanctuary, talks to individuals in the pews, makes a lot of eye contact. Her voice is forceful and energetic, and she's funny. "Our congregation was laughing, nodding, and very much with her every moment," says Mitzi Henderson, P-FLAG's fourth president and an elder in a Palo Alto Presbyterian church where Jane has been a visiting minister.

However spellbinding she is as a preacher, Jane finds her principal fulfillment in pastoral care, in bringing her bountiful compassion to those in need. It was to fill such a role that parishioners of the Downtown Presbyterian Church in Rochester, New York, issued her the call that touched off the denominational firestorm in 1991.

She was chosen by a vote of some 90 percent of the congregation's eight hundred members to become one of four pastors at the church. But ten other Presbyterian churches in the area filed a protest with denomination authorities; the ensuing litigation focused national attention on Jane and the Presbyterians.

The specific issue in Jane's case was narrow and technical. In 1978, the Presbyterian church had banned the ordination of openly gay ministers. The ruling contained an exemption for those ordained before 1978, and Jane was ordained in 1974. Nevertheless, her opponents argued, the 1978 ruling barred her from actually serving as a pastor.

The case pitted entrenched authority against the advocates of a more open, inclusive, and tolerant church. The size of the chasm between the factions was revealed by the votes of the denominational bodies that heard the case. The Northeast Synod Judicial Commission upheld Jane's call by a nine-to-one vote—but was then reversed by an eleven-to-one vote of the General Assembly's Permanent Judicial Commission.

The gulf between the factions was (and remains) vast. Consider the contrasting frames of reference by which the matter of Jane's sexuality was judged. First, the lawyer for the ten Rochester churches, Julius Popinga:

> We need to be explicit without embarrassing each other. We're not talking about homosexual orientation, we're not talking about proclivities, tendencies. We're talking about tactile, reciprocal, erotic, genital stimulation between or among persons of the same sex.

Now listen to Jane:

> God yearns for us to be ourselves. Being true to my orientation is the most spiritual thing that ever happened to me. The same place where I feel Coni, where I feel drawn to her, is where I feel God. We call it "sexu-spiritual." I love Jim, but with Coni, it's like I've come home. It's the most wonderful, peaceful, passionate relationship.

Where Popinga and his kind look and see smut, other people, such as Jane, find integrity, beauty, love—and God.

In key respects, the church's stance resembles that of the military's "don't ask, don't tell" policy regarding gay service personnel. It doesn't bar all gay and lesbian pastors, only those who are "self-avowed and unrepentant": only those, like Jane, who are honest about it. In Rochester, for example, Presbyterians have been quoted as saying they know of at least five gay ministers in their denomination in their area alone.

The Presbyterian church, of course, is not alone among American denominations in this seeming hypocrisy. Why do churches and synagogues persist in barring their priesthoods to such dedicated, capable, inspirational persons as Jane Spahr?

One possible factor is that organized religion remains a principal bulwark of male dominance in society. Open approval of homosexuality, with its inherent challenge to established gender roles, poses an obvious threat. This is apparently what one writer covering Jane's trial, Joan Lambert, had in mind when she wrote of Jane: "The patriarchy is petrified. Here's a woman who not only engages in homosexual behavior, she *crows* about it."

But the price is high. How many highly qualified ministers do churches lose because, unlike Jane, they are unwilling to serve an institution that denies their integrity? What is the cost to its own honor when such an institution engages in blatant hypocrisy? What are the lessons it teaches its congregants?

And, critically, what do such policies say to the churches' young gay members? Again, Joan Lambert puts this in perspective. Recalling the suicide of Bobby Griffith, which appeared to be tied so closely to the anti-gay teachings of his Presbyterian church, she writes:

> Maybe Julius Popinga is right—perhaps we *should* be explicit when discussing this issue: We are talking about teenagers who take razors and slice open the veins of their wrists. They take pills, or use guns. They hang themselves in their bedroom for their parents to find them. We get the picture.

If, as Jane says, her openness about her sexuality has brought her inner peace and passion, the outer turmoil it provoked was perhaps equally inevitable. Long before it was to cost her the Rochester post that seemed so tailor-made for her, it had caused her the loss of two other jobs. A San Rafael church eased her out as assistant minister after she told the head minister she was a lesbian. She then moved to Oakland as executive director of that city's Council of Presbyterian Churches; but that job too was cut short when her sexual orientation became an issue. Jim was enraged at this, and he made certain the local media reported the matter. "The person I loved so very much, the mother of my children, was being spat on again by the organization that's supposed to be about love," he says.

Her lesbianism now a public matter, Jane for more than a decade thereafter ran the Ministry of Light, later known as Spectrum, a social service organization for lesbians and gay men in Marin county.

Largely because of the church's rejection of Jane, and the underlying bias it reflects, Jim and Jackie now take a dim view of organized religion. Recently, they appeared with Jane, Jimmy, and Chet at a P-FLAG convention workshop; Jane was the only one of the five to express a desire to retain contact with the church. Jackie told the gathering, "Forgive me folks, I don't mean to hurt anyone, but I think the church needs to die and be resurrected from the ashes. I have a spiritual place in my heart that grieves for it." Jim said he is personally "Christian through to my toes" but, "I can't go to the church, any church." Instead, he says, P-FLAG provides "the safe place, the island I need to go to every now and then to recharge." And Jimmy, speaking for himself and Chet, asks, "When you look at what this is doing to our mom, do you really expect us to go and throw something in your offering cups?"

But Jane, despite its rejection of her, has never considered leaving the church. Even as a child—when she "thought God and I were pals"—she says she knew that being a Presbyterian minister was her calling. So when the Rochester liaison fell through, she simply shifted her focus. Backed privately by ardent admirers within the denomination, she became the church's first "evangelist educator," championing acceptance of lesbians and gay men within the church. She is booked for speaking engagements at least two years in advance.

"I want this church to be a safe place for people to talk about what they need to talk about," she says. "I want to help change any system that encourages people to keep secrets. Secrets kill you from the inside out.

"We have to convey that being gay or lesbian is an incredibly spiritual thing. I will not listen to any church tell us any more that we are not spiritual people. We heard the 'yes' inside us when the culture said 'no,' and that had to do with our deep inside which is our spirituality. When you come home to yourself, you've come home to a faith that is incredible, whether you call it a higher power or whatever. I worry for the church because it can lose its heart and its soul if it does not come to know who we are."

On that score, Jane has a soulmate in Mel White, one-time best-selling ghost-writer for such stalwarts of the religious right as Jerry Falwell, Pat Robertson, Billy Graham, and Oliver North. White, an ordained minister, lost favor with his colleagues after coming out in 1984. Ten years later, he wrote *Stranger at the Gate*, a highly publicized book of his experiences. His ex-wife, Lyla, wrote a moving foreword to the book in which she made clear that she has never doubted their mutual love. (Like the Spahrs, the Whites remain close and share family holidays with their two sons and granddaughter.)

White says the reason he is now shunned by Falwell, Robertson, and the others is that they fear the truth. For one thing, he says, gays and lesbians are physically present "at the heart" of the nation's churches. "We lead their choirs and we play their organs and we're their deacons and board members, and we have more than our share of pastors and priests and rabbis," he told Morley Safer on *60 Minutes*.

Echoing Jane's point, White said, "The closet is a place of death for gay people. Coming out is a place of life."

Wayne and Sandra Schow

Bishop Wheatley says a prayer of thanks to God "for sending those gay children to us." I've heard the same gratitude expressed over and over by parents of gay kids. Jane Doherty, the stepmother of Ian MacNeil (see Chapter 11), puts it quite bluntly: "I'm so much happier that Ian is gay than I would be if he weren't."

At first blush, nevertheless, it's difficult to believe that Wayne and Sandra Schow of Idaho would be among the ranks of the grateful. Their son, Bradley, was the first person in his state to die of AIDS.

Preston, Idaho is a farm town of 3,500 souls in picturesque Cache Valley in the southeast corner of the state. It was there, alongside the Bear River and ringed by a majestic stretch of the Rocky Mountains, that Wayne and Sandra Schow met and became high school sweethearts. Three miles down Highway 91 is a massive road sign announcing the site in foot-high letters as the "Birthplace of Ezra Taft Benson." Nationally, Benson was best known as one of President Eisenhower's cabinet members. But here, less than two hours north of the Mormon Tabernacle in Salt Lake City, he is revered for his decades-long incumbency, ending with his death in 1994, as First President (the "prophet, seer, and revelator") of the 8.7-million-strong Church of Latter Day Saints.

Wayne says that Mormonism was a force "whose outlook and values and political power dominated all aspects" of his and Sandra's early lives. Their families had been Mormon for generations. Virtually all of their relatives lived in either Idaho or Utah, where cultural, commercial, and media influences radiated wholly from Salt Lake City. Shortly after high school graduation,

Wayne spent thirty months in Denmark on a church proselyting mission.

Wayne and Sandra were married in the church's Logan Temple shortly after he returned from Denmark. Wayne undertook a scholarly career that led to his current position as chair of the English Department at Idaho State University in Pocatello, less than an hour's drive north of Preston. There, they raised four sons in the same rigorous Mormon tradition; three of the boys ultimately fulfilled foreign proselyting missions.

To be raised as a Mormon, Wayne has written, "is to be subjected to a formidable process of indoctrination, Sunday School, Primary, Aaronic Preisthood activity, daily seminary instruction during high school years, a variety of special worship services, and youth conferences." In this way, he says, the faith "absorbs one's time and attention"; it claims to have "answers for virtually all of life's great questions." And the inevitable answer regarding homosexuality is "No!"

Brad, oldest of the four Schow sons, was born in 1958. He was a handsome, sandy-haired, gregarious boy with the broad-shouldered, slim-hipped, muscular build that suggested the strong swimmer he was. He played the piano well; he was a member of the church choir and during high school sang with a popular small group known as the Ambassadors. His broad circle of friends, drawn largely from his daily seminary classes, included both boys and girls, and a number of high school athletes. Sandra says he loved to have fun.

To his parents, though, it was Brad's wide-ranging intellectual interests and philosophical bent that was most striking about him. He had what Wayne calls a "sticky mind," with a sharp questioning streak and "a good BS detector." "It was wonderful how often I would lay on him some platitude and he would challenge me on it and force me to back up."

Brad had been aware since grade school that he was sexually attracted to males. He had a series of unspoken crushes on the basketball and football players who were his closest high school friends. He was beset, as his father later wrote, by "an inclination that was, in the context of his world, unthinkable."

Just before his twentieth birthday he told his parents he was gay. In retrospect, they say, they were woefully unprepared for the announcement.

"He knew, I am sure," Wayne says, "that we still did love him. But we could not say, 'Listen to the voice within you, Brad, and follow it. Go with our blessing: find and nourish who you really are.' We could not say it . . . How could we give him license to 'become' something we had been taught to abominate?"

Wayne was convinced that homosexuality stemmed from bad parenting or bad family relationships, and couldn't believe that applied to the Schows. He thought homosexuality had no place in any decent person's life—that "it was a choice, a bad choice, and perverse." So his initial reaction was that "this simply was not a possibility in our family"—that Brad was temporarily confused. He told his son to be patient, that the first time Brad experienced sex with a woman, "you're going to feel a lot different about this."

For her part, Sandra was initially overwhelmed by guilt. "Everything I read said it was my fault." And she knew that at church, she'd be told all she had to do was pray about it, "or that I needed to change something about myself."

Because he had not yet engaged in homosexual behavior, Brad was qualified to participate in the church's mission program. But breaking with family tradition, he concluded he could not do so without denying his identity. Shortly thereafter, in 1980, he made another fateful decision. He had found a gay companion who was moving to Los Angeles to enroll in a graduate program at UCLA; Brad decided to go with him.

Brad settled in West Hollywood, a virtually all-gay enclave where he participated in the easygoing lifestyle typical of gay communities prior to the mid-1980s. Wayne visited him there only briefly; but it was long enough for him to absorb his first important lesson from having a gay child. "Meeting his friends was a door opener," he says. "I found they were normal people. They were healthy human beings. They did interesting things."

Mostly through Brad, Wayne came to know homosexual people back home, including a number of his own students and some of his colleagues. Recalling that, his eyebrows lift in tribute to the pleasant surprise it brought: "They turned out to be among the brightest and most sensitive people I knew."

In 1983, Brad split up with his companion. He began to feel that the hedonistic culture of West Hollywood was incompatible with what he needed to do. As Wayne now analyzes it, Brad had started to realize that "underlying the extremes of gay life in West Hollywood was a deep-seated nihilism . . . an attempt to cover despair."

Brad entered a program at Utah State University in Logan, just south of Preston. He felt his roots were there in the mountain area he loved. But at the same time, he felt he was an outsider, cut off from the church, whose influence was pervasive in Logan, and unable like his classmates to look forward to having his own family. ("He loved children. He really wanted a family," Sandra says.)

But he was excited about his participation in Utah State's nationally reputed program in landscape architecture, and he thought he could put up with the hostile church-dominated environment long enough to get his degree. He persevered, toiling overtime to master the program's math requirements, where he had always had difficulty. He lived in a dormitory and during his second year was a resident assistant.

So what happened in 1985, after what his father calls "his almost monkish retreat to Northern Utah," was a cruel irony.

When he came to Pocatello that summer to help build a new family home, Brad was plainly ill. The AIDS virus, unknown when he moved to Los Angeles but apparently incubating in his blood since his time there, had begun its deadly work. He never returned to Logan, and instead spent the remaining year and a half of his life in the Pocatello home. It was a period of pain, struggle, grief, and frustration for both Brad and his parents—but a deeply meaningful growth experience as well.

Within a few weeks after his return that summer, he was hospitalized with a burst appendix, and again shortly thereafter with a postoperative infection. Blood tests indicated that he was HIV-positive. "A nurse took me out in the hallway and said, 'It's going to be a long, hard, slow death. You'd better get counseling,'" Sandra remembers.

They did not get counseling, and they told only a very few of their closest friends what was happening. "We were all in the closet," Wayne says. "We were trying to explain why our son was home, why he wasn't looking too well."

Silence was especially difficult for Sandra. At the time, she says, she felt she was going to burst open. In two instances, the pressure she felt led her to confide in friends. But, "They just couldn't handle it, and more or less dropped me."

A few months after his first hospitalization, Brad developed pneumocystis pneumonia. He said he didn't want to be hospitalized again; but his parents called an ambulance anyway when it was plain he was near death. Earlier, he had made clear he did not want to be kept alive by mechanical means; but Wayne and Sandra, unable to let him go, gave permission to put him on a respirator. And it seemed that Brad was not ready to let go, either. "Later we learned that without Brad's cooperation, the breathing tube could not have been efficiently inserted in the perilously short time left," Wayne says.

Brad survived, and even began to regain some weight. The Schows hoped for a medical breakthrough that would commute Brad's death sentence, but within another six months, his condition began to worsen rapidly. His muscles, nerves, and organs began to fail, and soon, even walking became intolerably painful. Brain lesions began to affect Brad's memory and eyesight. But his mind remained essentially clear, and he seemed to vacillate between wanting to die and wanting to live. He considered suicide, but decided to face out whatever came.

His last months were filled with philosophical discussions with his parents. He never gave up his arduous search for faith. But in the end, Wayne says, "However much solace traditional faith might have provided, he went as an agnostic to face whatever lies beyond."

From his perspective as a literary scholar, Wayne sees Brad as a classic tragic figure; and he has written thoughtfully and movingly on that theme. During Brad's final months, he says, "I felt like a member of a Sophoclean chorus, standing by watching something unfolding that was profoundly human, profoundly important. It was something larger than my understanding but that caused me to feel privileged to be thus challenged."

In one article, Wayne wrote, "[Brad] is not a large-scale tragic protagonist, to be sure. But in the pursuit of what he justly desired of life, in the face of forces inimical to his needs, he did not flinch or turn aside. . . . [H]e insisted on his right to *be*, to search after happiness and fulfillment according to the conditions thrust on him by his biology and his particular place and moment in history. . . . [T]he nemesis of AIDS came along as a by-product of his bold quest."

The essence of classical tragedy is a flawed protagonist, who in a losing confrontation with life's turns-of-chance achieves impressive stature and compels admiration. Tragedy, Wayne writes, "assures us there are some of our kind whose existential response to [life's] terrible dilemmas can, without embarrassment, be called great."

And so it is without embarrassment that Wayne now views his son's spirited but doomed confrontation with his own terrible dilemma. Brad wrestled with an insoluble conflict—that between his deepest sense of who he was, and a conscience formed by the church into which he was born. He met the challenge head-on, although in hindsight he made some decisions that were risky and impetuous. But Wayne observes that tragic individuals are not noted for prudence, and Brad's choices reflected his intense need to find moral and philosophical justification for the person he knew himself to be. He did not, as do many, surrender docilely, fearful of challenging his culture's prevailing order.

By any measure, Brad's life and death have unquestionably served one principal function of classic tragedy. They have provided inspiration to others: namely, Wayne and Sandra. And both are eloquent in assessing what Brad gave them.

Wayne says that sharing Brad's ordeal "enlarged our awareness of the human condition. . . . We learned so much from the courageous, independent and self-reliant way he faced his illness and his life. We are grateful to him; we are proud of him. He was such a fine young man.

"At this point, we can say we feel blessed to have had a son who was homosexual. It has taught me more about love. It has pushed me harder to broaden my philosophy. It has made me more aware of the complexity and ultimately the beauty of diversity in God's creation than anything I have otherwise experienced.

"It was an enormously rewarding experience to have had him in my life."

For Sandra, the experience enhanced a process of personal growth that led her to declare her independence from the church about the time of Brad's death.

"I'm sure a lot of people think I just kind of flipped out when Brad died, but that's not the case." Leaving the church, she says, was the result of a decades-long progression toward gaining her own sense of identity and self-confidence. Her serious questioning (a quest that Wayne says has helped him become something of a feminist) had begun even before Brad's disclosure of gayness. But the months culminating in Brad's death solidified her resolve.

"His example of trying to be who he was, at great odds, led me to decide I had to be authentic too," she says. "I had to learn not to live my life in fear. Fear of some kind of reprimand. Fear of some kind of judgment against me that would be made by friends, people within the church, or my family.

"It made me take personal responsibility for some powerful stands in my life. I had to meet the challenge of dealing with illness and death. But even more importantly, I had to face the kind of games I had been playing, in relinquishing my power to someone else to tell me what I ought to be doing."

One of the first things she did for herself was to refrain from attending her own son's wedding because of church regulations that Sandra was no longer willing to heed. Son Ted was married in the Temple in Salt Lake City, where admission is restricted to those in good standing with the church; such a certification is conditioned upon successful current completion of a two-stage "worthiness interview" with church officials. Sandra decided that she could no longer submit a decision on her worthiness to others. Her family, including Ted, understood.

The Schows are convinced that the homophobia to which theirs and other churches contribute robbed their son of a happier, more fulfilling life. They see anti-gay attitudes—which lower gays' self-esteem, deprive their relationships of the cement of social sanction, and drive them to hedonism—as responsible for much of the promiscuity that exists in segments of the gay community and might have contributed to Brad's death. "Brad's story could have been so different if we had been open to understanding, if we could have had our heads out of the sand," Sandra says.

Wayne has written extensively about the family's experience. He first came out, in fact, in a letter after Brad's death to one of the apostles of the church, arguing for greater church acceptance of homosexuality. Later, the letter was expanded into an article that caused a nationwide stir, both within and outside the church, when it was published in *Sunstone*, an independent Mormon journal. Since then, he has written other articles; co-edited a book, *Peculiar People*, an anthology of essays on religion and homosexuality by theologians and lay Mormons; and authored a book of personal reflections entitled *Remembering Brad.*

In matter-of-fact tones that seem to reflect long hours of meditation on the subject, Wayne expressed certain regrets to an interviewer last year:

"I wish I had the past sixteen years to live over. I would be able to do a lot better job of being a father to the son I loved so much. I would have been able to be a better friend to him. . . . I would have been able to help him accept himself. . . .

"I would have been able not just by my spoken words but by my willingness to come out and be public about his homosexuality . . . to build his confidence in himself."

His voice drops as he says more softly: "I would love to have an opportunity now to do that over. I wasn't a great success in meeting that challenge. I moved as fast as I could according to the bad information I had . . . .

"I could do a better job now."

10

◆

A Holocaust Survivor Confronts Homophobia

On a November evening a little more than two years after we first met Paulette Goodman, Myrna and I attended a black-tie event in the elegant Grand Ballroom of New York's Waldorf Astoria Hotel. At the head table, Paulette sat next to Elie Wiesel, Nobel Peace laureate and world-renowned chronicler of the Holocaust. They were both being honored with Humanitarian Awards from the Human Rights Campaign Fund, an organization dedicated to equality and justice for lesbians and gay men.

It was fitting for Paulette to share the spotlight with Wiesel. Both had lived through the Holocaust. And both were there that night largely because the persecution of lesbians and gay men evoked memories of that horrible era. In his keynote speech, Wiesel noted that gays shared with Jews the fate of Nazi death camps—that he personally had seen gays "in those places of darkness, silence, and fire."

He went on to supply the answer to a question on the minds of many of the eight hundred people present: Why would one of the most eminent scholars and writers of our age, himself from an orthodox religious background, accept an award from an organization of homosexual activists? "You need not be surprised,"

Wiesel said. "Those who hate you, hate me. Those who hate, hate everybody. So why should I not be here to speak to you about self-respect and about civil rights that must apply to every single segment of our population and to every area of human endeavors? . . . We are all human beings."

In accepting her own award on behalf of P-FLAG, of which she had been national president for the past year, Paulette cited her own memories of the Holocaust. She recalled her childhood in Nazi-occupied Paris, and told of the loss of numerous relatives in German death camps. To survive, she said, she had to hide the fact that she was a Jew: "I know how stifling it is to be in the closet."

Paulette was one of nine children of Polish parents who had moved to Paris when her father became an ironworker for the French national railroad. There, as a youngster during World War II, she was required to wear a Star of David on her clothing. Other children called her *sale Juive*, "dirty Jew."

Thus, as a young child, Paulette learned what it meant to be "different." Once a week, defying a Nazi order banning Jews from appearing in various public places, she would take off her Star of David and go with other children to the movies, "even though we knew that if we got caught, the whole family would have been wiped out."

She has no idea why most of her immediate family were spared the Gestapo dragnets that claimed aunts, uncles, nieces, nephews, and grandparents. But when the war ended, relatives in New York City helped Paulette, one sister, and two brothers emigrate there. Her parents were unable to obtain United States visas for themselves, and so moved to Montreal, where other relatives lived. The sixteen-year-old Paulette had never before been separated from her parents; and after three months in New York, she decided to move to Montreal to be with them. Then, nine days before her departure, she met Leo Goodman, a nineteen-year-old engineering student.

A series of obstacles plagued the ensuing courtship. The first was language. Paulette's English was still halting. They both understood Yiddish, having heard it regularly in their childhood homes—but neither could speak it. At first, they had to communicate largely by hand signals, but their affection for each other was nonetheless clear by the time Paulette moved to Montreal. Thereafter, daily exchanges of letters and frequent trips by Paulette to New York and Leo to Montreal—one for several months while he worked there as a draftsman and toolmaker—kept the relationship going.

They became engaged, only to worry in their youthful innocence about still another potential barrier. In moving to Canada, Paulette had relinquished her immigrant status in the United States. Hesitantly, during a visit to New York in 1951, they entered an immigration office. A clerk sternly advised them that while wives of U.S. citizens were allowed in the country, mere betrothal conferred no standing whatever on Paulette. They were crestfallen. But the clerk winked. "It's simple," he said. "Just get married." Three days later, on a hot summer afternoon, they were married in the living room of a Yonkers judge. (Paulette didn't consider herself "really married" until a rabbi performed a second ceremony some months later in a relative's home in Montreal.)

Paulette and Leo have now been together more than forty years, and have two children and two grandchildren. Until the early 1980s, Paulette's energies went almost entirely into her family. She thought of herself as an old-fashioned homemaker, and had few outside interests. Then, while living in Maryland, where Leo worked as a research scientist, they learned one of their children was gay.

Paulette, more distressed than Leo by the revelation, found a support group composed of a handful of other parents and a few gay men. As she learned about homosexuality and the irrational animosity it aroused, she was reminded of the bigotry and hatred the Nazis had engendered.

As a child wearing her Star of David, Paulette had been

unaware of the Nazi oppression of gays. Between 1933 and 1945, the Germans arrested as many as 100,000 gay men, jailed some 60,000, and sent 10,000 to 15,000 to concentration camps. In the prisons and camps, gays wore pink triangles on their sleeves. Like the Jews' yellow Star of David, it was homosexuals' particular badge of disgrace and dishonor. (Today, it carries a very different meaning; it has become the worldwide symbol of the gay liberation movement.)

The United States Holocaust Memorial Museum in Washington, D.C. is now recording the Nazi treatment of gays by collecting documents, photographs, and artifacts; it is perhaps the world's first museum to include memorabilia of the gay community in a scholarly exhibit. Collecting the material is complicated by the reluctance of most survivors even now to speak of their experiences with researchers; apparently, they still find it difficult to think of themselves as anything other than common criminals. For one thing, in the wake of World War II, Germany was swept by moral crusades fueled by appeals to so-called family values, and many of the gay Holocaust survivors reportedly were again arrested and imprisoned.

But Nazi persecution of gays was still unknown to Paulette in 1983, when she found herself edging into a leadership role in the fight against American prejudice. In that year, she and Leo decided to organize their little support group into the Washington-area chapter of P-FLAG. She wanted Leo to be the first president, but he demurred and no one else stepped forward; by default, the position fell to Paulette.

Her activist career was launched, but it had a slow start. For the second time in her life, she found herself closeted. She shunned publicity of any sort. Although chapter meetings were held at her house, she never told her neighbors why all these people were visiting her. (She let them assume that the Goodmans gave a lot of parties.) She remembers several occasions when, hearing a neighbor at the door, she frantically hid any books or literature that might give her away. "I would be absolutely beside myself," she says. "This is what it's like being in the closet."

Ultimately, she was outed by the media after the chapter decided to sponsor an ad campaign on city buses to seek new members. A county councilman objected to the plan, and suddenly P-FLAG was in the news. Paulette was called by a *Washington Post* reporter who had learned from a county document of her role as P-FLAG president. Once the *Post* article appeared, television cameras were at her door. This time, hiding the books and literature could not help!

In retrospect, she is grateful for the outing. As head of Washington P-FLAG, she was responsible for getting the word out to others who needed support: "How could we reach out to people if I was not able to speak openly?" As it happened, she found speaking out to be personally liberating; and few since have found Paulette Goodman short of words or camera-shy where the welfare of "our gay loved ones" is at stake.

She has spoken before state and local legislatures, been featured in scores of newspaper and magazine articles, and appeared on television and radio programs. She has led workshops at universities and churches, and at organizations (gay and non-gay) beyond count. On numerous occasions, she has gone jaw-to-jaw with anti-gay hardliners. Once, as television cameras whirred, she even debated a notorious anti-gay crusader, Reverend Joseph Chambers, on a city sidewalk.

That confrontation took place in 1991 in Charlotte, North Carolina, in front of the Omni Charlotte Hotel, site of that year's P-FLAG national convention. For months prior to the convention, through the media and the newsletter of his own organization known as Concerned Charlotteans, Chambers roused his supporters to a fever pitch of anti-gay sentiment. He told them that P-FLAG's pro-family stance was a facade designed "to fool the public and hide its immoral deeds." The use of convention name tags, he said, was "a slick plan so homosexuals can make contact for sodomy sex." He also claimed that the inverted pink triangle was an occult symbol "frequently denoting the unholy trinity of Satan, the Antichrist, and the false prophet."

During the convention itself, Chambers's followers picketed the hotel with signs proclaiming, "The homosexual conference is not telling you the truth." Paulette happened to pass the picketers one afternoon when Chambers himself was present, and her temper flared. Within moments, the woman who not long before had hidden P-FLAG literature from her neighbors was surrounded by television cameras and reporters as she denounced Chambers to his face. Charlotte viewers heard her on that night's newscast, sharply informing Chambers that it was anti-gay bigotry, not P-FLAG, that was destroying families.

Of all her accomplishments, Paulette is probably proudest of the part she has played in educating mental health professionals on behalf of misunderstood gay and lesbian children. She has spoken, for example, at annual meetings of both the American Psychiatric Association and the American Academy of Child and Adolescent Psychiatry. It is the plight of lesbian and gay youth, evoking visions of her own frightened and closeted childhood, that now concerns her most.

Starting in 1988, Paulette led national P-FLAG during four years of mushrooming growth. When she took the reins, the organization was a loose confederation of local groups run out of her Maryland kitchen. When she stepped down in 1992, P-FLAG was a national presence with more than three hundred chapters and hotlines in twelve countries, all administered by a professional staff in Washington, D.C.

During her tenure, while a conservative Republican administration was in power, she obtained recognition and support for P-FLAG from within the White House itself. The incident, which triggered angry remonstrances from the conservative wing of the Republican Party, reveals both Paulette's generosity of heart and her doggedness of purpose.

In 1989, impressed by the apparent warmth of First Lady Barbara Bush, Paulette wrote her a letter "mother-to-mother." In it, she asked Mrs. Bush to "speak kind words to some 24 million gay Americans and their families, to help heal the wounds, and to keep these families in loving relationships." Paulette was keenly disappointed when she received nothing more than a routine acknowledgment from a White House aide.

In April 1990, however, Paulette decided to try another tack. She and I were among those attending the signing of the Hate Crimes Statistics Act by President Bush, and Paulette brought along a copy of the 1989 letter. She asked me whether I thought she should give it to one of the White House staffers with the request that it be hand-delivered to Mrs. Bush.

"No harm in trying," I told her, although I wondered why she would want to waste her energy in such a patently useless way. After all, Bush was no political novice, and her husband had been elected on a strongly conservative platform.

Paulette followed her optimistic instincts, and ten days later received a note on White House stationery. "You sound like a caring parent and a compassionate citizen," the First Lady began, and then added the words that warmed the hearts of P-FLAGgers around the country:

> I firmly believe that we cannot tolerate discrimination against any individuals or groups in our country. Such treatment always brings with it pain and perpetuates hate and intolerance. I appreciate so much your sharing the information about your organization and your encouraging me to help change attitudes. Your words speak eloquently of your love for your child and your compassion for all gay Americans and their families.
>
> With all best wishes, warmly, Barbara Bush.

The First Lady's gracious reply soon came to the attention of conservative Republicans, who immediately attacked the White

House. According to syndicated columnists Robert Novak and Rowland Evans, the critics found Mrs. Bush's simple expression of fair play to be an "outrage." The columnists described "Republican politicians and worried White House aides" as being concerned that the letter had "pushed the Bush agenda into political danger." Paulette herself was described in the column as a "gay-lobby activist."

But Paulette had the last word, in remarks quoted in several newspapers, including the *Washington Post* and *Chicago Sun-Times*. Far from being a gay-lobby activist, she said, "I am simply the mother of two wonderful children, one of whom happens to be gay, and a volunteer in an organization dedicated to keeping families together.

"It was in those roles that I wrote Mrs. Bush, and she responded in a caring and nonpolitical vein. She apparently realizes that it is society's discrimination against our kids—and not their innate sexual orientation—that truly threatens family structures."

The undoubted apex of Paulette's P-FLAG experience came after she retired as national president. On April 23, 1993, the United States Holocaust Memorial Museum was dedicated in the nation's capital. (Appropriately, the dedication occurred during the week of a massive march on Washington for gay civil rights.) The speaker representing P-FLAG was the woman who remembered having to remove her Star of David in order to go to the movies with other children in Paris.

As at the dinner in New York with Elie Wiesel two years earlier, Paulette compared her Holocaust experience with that of gays everywhere. "I and other French Jewish children had to fool the Christians so that we could survive," she said. "So I was denied my Yiddishkeit [Jewish identity]. Because of prejudice and oppression, I was not proud of being a Jew. But now I am proud to be a Jew, proud to be the parent of a gay child, and proud to be a member of P-FLAG.

"At first, when I found out I had a gay child, I found myself in a closet again, just as my child had been before coming out to us. So I realize the prejudice gay, lesbian, bisexual, and transgender people are living through. It did not take me long to see the parallels. Oppression and prejudice and persecution are the same wherever they occur."

The dedication crowd cheered in agreement. And it chanted, "Never again! Never again! Never again!"

Could such a thing as the Holocaust happen again? I have a friend who thinks it could—here in America, to gays.

My friend, a gay man who frequently attends P-FLAG meetings in an eastern city, was born in a small town in Germany in 1930, three years before Hitler seized power. Although baptized in the Lutheran faith of his mother, he had a Jewish father. He vividly remembers "Kristallnacht"—November 9, 1938—the night that his middle-class home and his childhood innocence were trashed by Nazis and Hitler Youth. The invaders smashed furniture, mirrors, pictures, doors, and windows as the terrorized eight-year-old stood on the stairway beside his stunned mother. The next day at school, his once-friendly classmates jeered and taunted him. His parents told him he must never again enter their homes. Soon thereafter, the family escaped Germany and came to the United States.

At P-FLAG meetings, my friend warns parents of a parallel between the Nazis' obsession with genetic purity and American fundamentalists' belief that homosexuality can be treated or cured. He tells them they should wonder whether the day might come when their children—and they themselves, in light of evidence that gayness might be genetically influenced—would be ordered to hospitals for sterilization. Or when, as he once wrote, "hordes of state-sanctioned punks could break into your homes to take away your loved ones because they are gay."

American history and traditions establish very long odds

against such horrors. But the understandable fears of a gay Nazi survivor are instructive. For the evil nature of prejudice, and its potential for violence, are generic, whoever the target. Nazis incited Germans with wild anti-Semitic claims: for example, that Jews drink the blood of Christian babies. American anti-gay radicals resort to similar absurdities: for instance, that homosexuality is associated with pedophelia and bestiality.

Nor are these casual slogans. In 1994, when the Oregon Citizens Alliance unveiled a second statewide measure to outlaw legal protections for gays, they called it the "Child Protection Act." And in the ensuing campaign, the OCA actually charged that Nazism grew out of Germany's gay rights movement! According to OCA leaders, the Nazi party "began in a homosexual bar," and all of its evils could be traced to "the minds and perverted ideas of homosexuals."

Some Oregonians were stunned by the blatant demonstration of raw bigotry. But not my German friend. Not Paulette Goodman. And not, presumably, Elie Wiesel. They understand the incendiary potential of common prejudice.

11

•

Public Figures and Their Gay Relatives

" I don't know any gay people." You hear it often, but the speaker is almost certain to be wrong. Aware of it or not, the average person encounters lesbians and gay men almost every day.

"We are everywhere" is a slogan of the gay community, and it reflects a significant demographic truth. Sexual orientation is wholly independent of race, class, nationality, social standing, education, or religious or political ideology. As nearly as can be determined, homosexuality has occurred in roughly the same proportion in all societies, and at all levels, throughout history.

So it is hardly surprising that families of the famous are no more immune to gayness than any other. Within the gay community, it is common knowledge that families with gay members include leading figures in politics (extending to former occupants of the White House), entertainment, business, the professions, and the arts. For the most part, for a variety of professional and personal reasons, these families have remained in the closet. But it is perhaps a sign of growing social maturity that in recent years, a number of public figures have spoken out in support of gay family members. Among them are two distinguished longtime members of the Senate, one of the most highly respected figures of broadcast journalism, a secretary of commerce in the Bush administration, a California congresswoman, a leading theater impresario, and a federal judge.

Ideally, of course, a family member's gayness should be no more noteworthy than his or her eye color. Someday, that will be the reality. Meanwhile, as we in P-FLAG struggle for our children's equality, we are grateful to these public figures whose forthright-ness is helping speed that day's arrival.

Robert Mosbacher

Robert Mosbacher's role as supportive father of a lesbian daugh-ter hit the news in 1991, when both he and his daughter happened to deliver commencement speeches at southern California colleges on the same day. Dr. Diane "Dee" Mosbacher began her speech by saying: "Dad and I had breakfast this morning. We had a look at each other's speeches. He would have used mine, but he's not a lesbian. I would have used his, but I am not a Republican."

Since "Dad" was then George Bush's secretary of commerce, newspapers around the country played up the quote. Asked to comment, Mosbacher issued a statement. Dee, he wrote, "is my daughter and I love her." He acknowledged that they didn't always see things the same way. But "I am proud of her for what she is, and I hope she feels that way about me."

One of the responses to the news coverage came from President Bush, who commended Mosbacher for supporting his daughter. The Bushes and Mosbachers are decades-old friends. Growing up in Houston, Dee had played touch football with the future presi-dent and lived across the street from one of his close friends, Jim Baker, Bush's secretary of state and chief of staff.

Dee now lives in San Francisco with Nanette Gartrell, her mate of twenty years and, like Dee, a psychiatrist. For several years into the early 1990s, Dee was regional medical chief for mental health in San Mateo county, south of San Francisco. Nanette was the first openly lesbian faculty member at Harvard Medical School, where she was a professor for eight years before joining the University of California medical faculty in San Francisco in 1987.

Gracing a table in a corner of their living room is a picture of the two women flanking President Bush, with Robert at Dee's side. The handwriting at the bottom says, "To Nanette, Best Wishes, George." The photograph and its inscription mask a central irony within the Mosbacher clan. For years, it was Dee's generally leftist politics, more than her sexual orientation, that most ruffled family calm. In the 1970s, for example, her sponsorship of antiwar rallies disturbed her father more than her lesbianism did. And the Mosbachers have always warmly welcomed Nanette at family gatherings, where she's referred to as Dee's spouse. That's been the term of preference since a 1989 White House reception where Dee introduced Nanette to Barbara Bush and Jim and Susan Baker as her lover. Robert suggested that *spouse* was more appropriate—*lover* simply didn't reflect the multifaceted quality of the women's relationship.

But in 1992, being openly lesbian in a family of conservative Texas Republicans became a tough juggling act. That year, Robert left the cabinet to become Bush's national campaign manager and later its chief fundraiser, while Dee's brother Rob headed the President's Texas campaign. It was also the year in which gays became high-profile GOP targets, and eventually Dee found herself publicly challenging the political loyalties of her father and brother.

The campaign season actually began on a note of friendly family cooperation. Dee asked her father if a campaign official could meet with gay activists; he said he'd do it himself. So he spent an hour with five representatives of the National Gay and Lesbian Task Force; and they talked about a range of issues including a proposed gay civil rights bill, discrimination against gays in the military, and AIDS.

The event, billed as the first meeting ever between gay leaders and the head of a President's re-election campaign, received broad media coverage. And it evoked sharp rebukes from the right. A group that included Representative Newt Gingrich of Georgia fired off an angry letter to Bush, calling the meeting "a slap in the face to every voter who affirms the traditional family." Bush himself, through his press secretary, denied personal knowledge of the meeting.

Dee was furious—the politicians had hung her father out to dry. "They had the audacity to say he is anti-family, when he's been fully supportive of his family."

After the Republican convention, though, Dee's anger was redirected to the campaign in which her father and brother were playing prominent roles. At the convention, gays were pilloried. Pat Buchanan declared a "cultural war" with gays as the enemy. Other speakers, such as the Christian Coalition's Pat Robertson, similarly vilified gays in pious references to "family values." The convention floor swarmed with placards reading "Family Rights Forever/Gay Rights Never." Barbara Bush was persuaded to remove an AIDS awareness ribbon she was sporting.

Although Dee values her privacy and rarely gives interviews, she now agreed to speak with Laura Blumenfeld of the *Washington Post*. A month before the election, her frustration was splashed over the front page of the *Post*'s Style section, in a lavishly illustrated article reprinted throughout the country.

"I would like my father to understand, I would like my brother to understand, I would like the Bushes to understand, that it's neither expedient nor ethical what they're doing," Dee was quoted. And Blumenfeld caught the broader irony reflected in the family's dilemma. Robert Mosbacher's plight, she wrote, was "[o]ne more chafing example of the divergence of political rhetoric and reality. . . . Preach Ozzie and Harriet till you're red, white, and blue in the face. But talk to just about anyone in American and they'll tell you about a cousin, an aunt, a brother who is gay, who is loved by his family."

Dee and Nanette had planned to host a major family reunion

on Thanksgiving, three weeks after the election. Invited were Robert and his wife Georgette (Dee's mother died in 1970), Rob, younger sisters Kathi and Lisa, a gaggle of nieces and nephews, and Nanette's family. However, the tension caused by the campaign scuttled the festivities. A coolness developed between Dee and the Mosbacher males.

But the chill would thaw. And P-FLAG would have a hand in restoring family amity.

For years, Dee had been a part-time filmmaker; and in 1993, with P-FLAG assistance, she produced *Straight from the Heart*, a video portraying families supportive of gay children. (In 1995, the documentary was nominated for an Academy Award.) By happenstance, she was invited to show it at a Houston conference, co-sponsored by P-FLAG, on the afternoon of her father's birthday. The conference crowd gave her a standing ovation. But the reception from a later private showing warmed her spirits even more. She played it for her father, and he was visibly moved. It seemed to give him a new appreciation of gay concerns. Father-daughter tensions eased. And afterward, the entire Mosbacher clan joined in a joyous birthday celebration at Robert's favorite restaurant.

Robert MacNeil

In a profession increasingly caught up in a tabloid mentality, the *MacNeil-Lehrer NewsHour* is a sober, articulate, intelligent holdout. Unafraid to sacrifice pizzazz for depth and insight, it is the undisputed monarch of serious broadcast journalism.

The command post of television's most distinguished news show is a modest book-lined office overlooking Manhattan's West Fifty-Seventh Street. One summer day in 1994 Myrna and I were privileged to visit there with Robert MacNeil and his son Ian. In a few hours, MacNeil would be reviewing the major events of the day for millions of viewers, and interviewing one of the astronomers who discovered the comet whose fragments had that day struck Jupiter. But now, relaxing in shirt sleeves, the *NewsHour's* executive editor drew attention to a book lying on his desk.

It was a copy of *The Family Heart*, P-FLAGger Robb Forman Dew's stirring memoir of her son's coming out. And the MacNeils were sharing their own coming out story.

In the rich tones that eased his way to the top ranks of broadcast journalism, MacNeil told us a story not unlike those regularly heard from P-FLAG parents. He described how Ian's revelation helped him be more honest with himself in a personal life crisis. And the stern visage familiar to millions took on an unwonted cast of pride and warmth as he cited Ian's own professional triumphs.

Robin, as he is generally known, spent much of his early career in England, where Ian was born and now, at thirty-four, has become the toast of international show business. Ian's set for the revival of *An Inspector Calls* won an Olivier, the British equivalent of a Tony, and later drew raves in a hit New York run. ("Dazzlingly original" was *Playbill* magazine's description of the set in its July 1994 lead story.)

Some months earlier, father and son had sat for a *New York Times* interview that marked the first time they had together publicly addressed Ian's gayness. Robin says that he has "no desire to be a campaigner on this issue." But he realizes his celebrity status confers special significance to a father's otherwise ordinary declaration of love and support for his son. And he found himself virtually forced to speak out in 1993 to rebut charges leveled by playwright and AIDS activist Larry Kramer.

In a letter addressed to MacNeil, with copies sent to more than fifty other journalists, Kramer had accused Robin of downplaying *NewsHour* coverage of AIDS and gay issues because of embarrassment over having a gay son. Robin's reply, printed in *New York* magazine, called the charge wrong on both counts. It listed a string of *NewsHour* firsts on AIDS coverage—including the first-ever documentary on ACT-UP, which Kramer founded. And it unequivocally declared MacNeil's love for his son.

The incident led Robin to experience something of the glow so common to P-FLAGgers when their support triggers spontaneous shows of affection from gay gatherings. For him, it happened at the 1993 convention of the National Lesbian and Gay Journalists Association, where he sat on a panel with Dan Rather, Tom Brokaw, and Judy Woodward. The four were asked when they intended to "cross the threshhold" and become sensitive to gay issues.

When it came Robin's turn, he said, "I crossed the threshhold years ago," and told them about Ian and the Kramer charge. He said he not only loved Ian but was very proud of him; and he told them Ian had just won the Olivier. MacNeil is warmed by the memory: "Well, it got a big cheer from these people, and I felt very good about that."

He says that when Ian came out to him twelve years ago, it precipitated a moment of truth in his own life—his separation from his second wife, Jane Doherty, just seven days after they received the letter from Ian disclosing his gayness. For a while, Robin had been caught on the horns of a dilemma: the marriage was no longer working, but he worried about the impact of a divorce on their two younger children. He credits Ian's coming out with supplying the "clarifying thrust" that enabled him to face up to a difficult decision. "Most of us don't self-examine until we have to," he observes wryly. Robin is now remarried and Doherty, who as step-mother had raised Ian and an older sister along with her two younger children by Robin, lives in Portland, Maine, where she is active in gay rights causes.

Slimmer and shorter than Robin, Ian otherwise closely resembles his father. But he speaks more softly and quickly, in a clipped British accent, as he emphasizes the importance of a public figure saying, "I love my gay son."

Ian says he knew at an early age that he was "different" and had accepted even before puberty that he was attracted to men. Robin and Jane early suspected that, and their suspicions gelled when Ian as a teenager showed no interest in dating girls.

Still, when Ian came out at age twenty, Robin was anxious about the implications. "I wondered, is he going to have a happy and satisfying personal and emotional life, or will it be a risky life?" Then he attended an eight-and-a-half-hour production of *Nicholas Nickleby*, and the Dickens spell, as it had done for him before, clarified his thinking.

"I really did get the revelation in the middle of watching *Nickleby* in that all-day production, that none of that really matters. That's up to him. You love this kid, he's a wonderful person, he has his own life to sort out, and he'd sort it out the best way."

It was fitting that Robin's epiphany took place at a play, for love of the theater is a strong bond between father and son. Now sixty-four, Robin was an aspiring actor and playwright before turning to journalism. Before Ian was born, one of Robin's plays nearly made it to production at London's Royal Court Theater—where Ian now works and Ian's lover and collaborator, Steven Daldry, is artistic director.

Daldry won a 1994 Tony as director of *An Inspector Calls*, and Robin's blue eyes dance as he recalls the acceptance speech of the man he calls his son-in-law. Daldry had quickly ticked off a list of "thank yous" but paused when he came to Ian. He had three separate reasons for thanking Ian, he told the national television audience: he was Daldry's closest collaborator, he designed the *Inspector* set, and "he's my lover."

You can't be more out than that, father and son agree.

Claiborne Pell

On May 21, 1993, the U.S. Senate was debating what would become the first confirmation of an openly gay person to high federal position. At issue was President Clinton's nomination of San Francisco Supervisor Roberta Achtenberg to become an assistant secretary of the Department of Housing and Urban Development.

The appointment was opposed by a bloc of Republican senators whose principal objection was Achtenberg's openness as a lesbian.

Senator Jesse Helms of North Carolina expressed outrage that Achtenberg and her companion, San Francisco Judge Mary Morgan, had embraced and kissed during a San Francisco gay pride parade. (One newspaper said he referred to the nominee as "that damn lesbian," and added that if that made him look like a bigot, so be it.) Also denouncing Achtenberg on the Senate floor were Bob Dole and Nancy Kassebaum of Kansas, Missouri's Christopher Bond, and Mississippi's Trent Lott.

Among those rising to decry the nature of these attacks was Rhode Island Democrat Claiborne Pell. One of the body's most distinguished members, Pell, then seventy-four, ranked third in seniority and chaired the powerful Committee on Foreign Relations. His forebears included five members of Congress, one of whom, George Dallas, had also been James Polk's Vice President. Pell had been a member of the conference that created the United Nations, and had written and sponsored scores of important pieces of legislation. His name even became part of the national lexicon in 1980 when Congress officially named a block of higher-education subsidies "Pell grants" to recognize his role in creating them. He had been decorated by no fewer than twelve foreign countries, and received honorary degrees from forty-six colleges and universities.

Now, he told his colleagues, he had a personal reason for supporting this nomination. His daughter Julia was a lesbian and president of the Rhode Island Alliance for Gay and Lesbian Civil Rights; and he would not want to see Julia barred from a government job because of her sexual orientation. "I believe we should strive to let simple standards of fairness and equal treatment be our guide in examining all nominees that come before us," he said. "I know I would want to see my daughter treated fairly, if she were the nominee before us today."

The nomination was approved fifty-eight to thirty-one.

Julia, always exuberantly proud of her father, delighted in his floor comments that day. "Father is a low-key kind of guy, not a big talker, so when he does get up on the floor, people listen," she says.

Julia was thirty before she realized she was gay. She immediately told her family and had their full support from the beginning. For some years before the Achtenberg debate, Senator Pell on various occasions had publicly acknowledged Julia's lesbianism, but never before on the Senate floor.

Julia has been with her partner, an artist, for eleven years, and helped raise the latter's daughter, now nineteen and a college student. She and her partner, Julia says, are "just an old-fashioned happily married couple."

Joe Papp

Throughout the day of November 1, 1991, New York radio and television bulletins reported the death of a "giant of the theater, creator of Shakespeare in the Park and so much more." Lights were dimmed not only on Broadway, listeners were told—"they dimmed from Avon to Central Park."

Joe Papp's New York Shakespeare Festival had brought the Bard free to the public. His seven-theater complex known as the Public Theatre had provided opportunities for new playwrights, and had sent on to Broadway such hits as *A Chorus Line* and *Hair*. He had brought to the American public such stars as Meryl Streep, George C. Scott, Colleen Dewhurst, and James Earl Jones. The *Encyclopedia Britannica* calls him a "major innovative force in U.S. theater in the second half of the twentieth century." A *New York Times* reviewer called him "arguably *the* . . . dominant shaper of contemporary American theater."

In launching the Shakespeare Festival, Papp worked for little pay for many years and produced and directed most of the plays himself. To him, his greatest triumph was the festival's policy of providing free performances in various locations around the city, including Central Park. Opposing the notion were such legendary city powers as Parks Commissioner Robert Moses and powerful theater critic Walter Kerr. But even they had to bow before the sheer force of Papp's passion for Shakespeare and his egalitarian vision of the Elizabethan's lusty appeal to Everyman.

But if Shakespeare was a major dynamic of Joe Papp's life, a tone of Greek tragedy hovered over his lingering death. While himself terminally ill with prostate cancer, he helped nurse his son Tony, who was dying of AIDS. Tony died first, five months before his father. "When he told me about Tony's death, he let out a high-pitched, anguished cry. I had never heard that sound come out of anyone's mouth before," said actor Kevin Kline, as reported by Papp's biographer, Helen Epstein, in *Joe Papp: An American Life.*

Until his marriage to his fourth wife in 1976, Papp's private life was often stormy. His relationships with his five children tended to be irregular, except with Tony, who had chosen to live with his father after his parents separated in 1973. When Tony was small, Papp would sometimes leave work in the middle of the day to buy gifts for the boy. He spent long hours playing with Tony at home and at the family beach house. When he was older, Tony worked backstage in his father's productions, and later, Joe enthusiastically subsidized Tony's creative but unprofitable career as a jewelry designer.

In the theater business, Joe had long known and been friendly with gay people. By the mid-1980s, his company had lost at least twenty men to AIDS; and Papp produced Larry Kramer's *The Normal Heart,* a wake-up call about the tragedy of the disease. Gay staffers never saw any indication that he was uncomfortable around them, as though he neither knew nor cared who was gay.

Nevertheless, when Tony at age fifteen told his father he might be gay, Joe went through the same rites of passage that most parents experience. He later admitted that it was far more difficult to accept the gayness of his own child than of someone outside the family. At first, he simply wanted to deny it. Then he was upset.

Then he blamed himself. But his love for Tony ultimately led to acceptance and an enhanced closeness in their relationship. "I've learned not only to accept his gayness but to love him for it," he told the media. He said the experience "wiped out the last vestige of prejudice" he felt toward gay people.

One of the ways Joe demonstrated support for Tony was to become a major donor to New York's Hetrick-Martin Institute. The Institute conducts the Harvey Milk School and other programs that benefit gay youth; and Papp was drawn by the fact that its very existence told teenagers it's okay to be gay. When he allowed his name to be announced with a major donor group there, it was the impresario's way of coming out as a parent. "I want to show my affection for my son Tony, because I love him," he said. "And I want to convey a message to other parents who don't know how to deal with a child who is gay."

Lynn Woolsey

In 1992, in her first run for Congress, Lynn Woolsey captured a stunning 67 percent of the vote in California's Sixth Congressional District. In Washington, the first major policy issue to confront her was President Clinton's proposal to end the ban on gays in the military.

She knew she could not in good conscience avoid a major role in the fight against the ban. Twenty-five years earlier, as the human resources director of an electronics firm, she had worked to extend its anti-discrimination policy to sexual orientation. As an eight-year member of the Petaluma, California City Council, she had become known as a champion of civil rights. She had run for Congress on human rights issues and felt an obligation to a constituency generally liberal on social matters.

First, though, there was a private family matter to resolve.

Five years earlier, Woolsey's step-son Michael had told her he was gay. He had also told his father and sister. But Michael still was not out to his two brothers or his other relatives. Woolsey had scary visions of Michael being outed, and of her own efforts being politically ridiculed by charges that she was in the closet about having a gay son. But she left the decision about going public to Michael.

He not only agreed to do so, but joined her in Washington to lobby for repeal of the ban. In June, in conjunction with P-FLAG and other ban opponents, she and Michael appeared together at a nationally publicized press conference. They hugged and kissed for the cameras. Mother said she hoped her son could help put a "real face" on homosexuality for lawmakers. "Our family exemplifies what family values is all about," she said. "We are accepting, supporting, and loving of each other." Of Michael, she said simply, "We are proud of him." Michael called his mother's efforts "really wonderful—she's an incredible voice for civil rights, for our family values."

Ultimately, the lobbying proved fruitless: Congress adopted the "don't ask, don't tell" policy on gays in the military, characterized by gay-friendly forces as a step backward. In a floor speech denouncing the policy, Woolsey said, "The Pentagon proposal says being gay is incompatible with military service. But this proposal is incompatible with the Bill of Rights. . . . Let the military get on with its real job—defending the rights of citizens, not taking them away."

She subsequently introduced an ingenious piece of legislation that would reduce each year's Department of Defense budget by the amount it had spent the prior year on training, investigating, and discharging gay service members. The bill was bottled up in committee, but it served to focus a spotlight on the immense sums wasted on such military witch hunts. (The government estimates it spends $27 million a year just for the recruiting and training costs of discharged gays.) She is also an original co-sponsor of the Gay and Lesbian Youth Suicide Prevention Act, which would establish a commission on gay youth within the Department of Health and Human Services.

Lynn raised Michael from age six along with her other two sons and daughter. She was the first in the family ("I was honored," she says) to whom Michael came out. His ultimate disclosure to the entire family, she says, created a positive new family dynamic of openness.

The reaction among her constituents? Mostly positive, but with an unusual twist. A number of people in Petaluma who say they are unbothered by Michael's gayness nevertheless complained about having learned of it through the newspapers. That has spawned an ongoing family joke, with a scenario featuring Michael going door-to-door in the time-honored campaign style of his mother. Woolsey laughs as she pictures it: "Can't you see him knocking on the door and announcing, 'Hello, I'm Michael Woolsey and I'm gay!'"

Lynn and Michael together addressed the 1994 P-FLAG convention in San Francisco. There, Lynn said of her son, "I am so proud of him. He is my friend, my ally. He's my partner in politics. And most of all, he's my son. I think everybody ought to have a Michael Woolsey in their life."

A. Wallace Tashima

For lawyers who practice in the federal courts of the Far West, the reference work of choice is *Federal Civil Procedure Before Trial*, co-authored by Judge A. Wallace Tashima. The two-volume work is a measure of the quality craftmanship that has graced a distinguished three-decade legal career.

Tashima was appointed a federal district judge in California's Central District by President Carter in 1980. Earlier, he had served as a deputy state attorney general, litigation and managing partner of the Los Angeles office of a national law firm, and a member of the state Committee of Bar Examiners. As a judge, his more than one hundred written opinions form a substantial body of law ranging over virtually every area of business, constitutional, and criminal law. He has lectured on the American legal system in such farflung spots as Egypt, Japan, and Myanmar.

The father of two sons and a daughter, Judge Tashima describes his reaction as "not positive but not grim" when his youngest child, Jonathan, disclosed he was gay in 1989. Like many parents, he had always thought of homosexuality as being abnormal. He now accepts gayness as "within the norm," but says he is still not completely comfortable with it. Even so, the Tashimas are a close-knit family, all fully supportive of Jonathan. His mother, Kiyo, is the most demonstrative: anti-gay comments in her presence inevitably draw an angry rebuttal. And whatever the remnants of the judge's own discomfort, he volunteered to go public in this book out of a conviction that Jonathan "has the right to live his life, like anyone else."

Tashima's sensitivity to the issue has also been raised by the law clerks he has employed, at least three of whom have been gay. They have helped him realize that they are "just human beings" whose sexual orientation does not affect their legal talents.

Such influence by law clerks does not stop with Judge Tashima. Although the clerks function primarily as legal researchers, they also serve as judges' sounding boards in wide-ranging discussions of social and legal issues, and write drafts (and sometimes the final versions) of court opinions. So the relatively traditional thinking of sitting judges may at times be shaped by the often more progressive perspective of their clerks.

Judge Tashima recalls in particular one of his own clerks whose partner worked for one of Tashima's older, quite conservative colleagues. The two young men, now in successful private practice, have since adopted two children; and Tashima is convinced that knowing them has opened the eyes of the older judge.

*　　*　　*

Barry Goldwater

To Barry Goldwater, the devil's name is Hypocrisy. His forthright-ness and stubborn integrity arguably cost him the American pres-idency because he refused to sugar-coat his views. But his uncom-promising honesty gained him the status of conscience of the Republican party and won him the respect and affection of the country he served for thirty-seven years in the Senate. And in his mid-eighties, it has led him to speak out fiercely on behalf of gay rights, a social movement founded on honesty and integrity.

If you are surprised at Goldwater's devotion to gay rights, you shouldn't be. It fits snugly into the character of this super-patriot, passionate political partisan, and outspoken exemplar of rugged individualism.

Like so many public figures, Goldwater has relatives—he men-tions a grandson and a grandniece—who are gay. But unlike so many public figures, he refuses to duck the issue. His relatives are vulnerable to unfair treatment by society, which makes the matter of political as well as personal significance. So an issue that oth-ers find awkward and confusing is, to Goldwater, crystal clear. People should be judged on their merit—period.

"Gays and lesbians are part of every American family. They should not be shortchanged in their efforts to better their lives and serve their countries," he has written. "It's time America realized that there was no gay exemption in the right to 'life, liberty, and the pursuit of happiness' in the Declaration of Independence."

Hence, when President Clinton made his ill-fated proposal to end the ban against gays in the military in 1993, Goldwater—a for-mer fighter pilot and Air Force general—backed the commander-in-chief in a widely quoted op-ed piece. "Everyone knows that gays have served honorably in the military since at least the time of Julius Caesar. They'll still be serving long after we're all dead and buried. But most Americans should be shocked to know that while the country's economy is going down the tubes, the military has wasted a half-billion dollars over the past decade chasing down gays and running them out of the armed services."

The next year, he was just as outspoken in favor of proposed federal legislation to ban employment discrimination against gays. He cited traditional Republican party principles for the proposition that in a free market economy, "competition and the Constitution matter—and sexual orientation shouldn't."

Goldwater once was a staunch defender of the ultra-conservative John Birch Society. But in 1994, he told an interviewer that the radical right is now spearheaded by "moneymaking ventures" bent on turning his party into a religious organization. If they succeed, he said, "kiss politics goodbye."

Since leaving the Senate in 1987, Goldwater has lived in retirement in his home overlooking Phoenix. Locally, he has lent his support to measures designed to outlaw discrimination in hiring based on sexual orientation. And in the fall of 1994, he signed on as honorary co-chair (with Oregon's retiring Governor Barbara Roberts) of a national gay rights campaign called Americans Against Discrimination. The campaign is sponsored by the Human Rights Campaign Fund, the leading gay lobbying organization; it was formed to back a federal anti-discrimination measure and fight the radical right's ubiquitous anti-gay initiatives. "I oppose the misuse of the initiative process by extremist groups to institutionalize discrimination," Goldwater said then. "Most people don't understand civil rights laws don't cover gay people and that gay people can be fired from their jobs."

His grandson, Ty Ross of Scottsdale, Arizona, who is close to the family patriarch, was quoted as saying of Goldwater, "He says, 'You people need to stand up for your rights.' One of those 'you people' kind of things."

Each year, gay Americans celebrate Coming Out Day on October 11, the anniversary of the 1987 march on Washington. The observance serves as a reminder not only to gay people but to their families and friends that the closet is an instrument of oppression; and all are encouraged to take some step toward the goal of total personal openness. For gay people, the step can be as small as attending their first meeting of a gay organization, or as big as coming out to their parents or their colleagues. For family members and friends, it might mean displaying some symbol of support of the gay movement, such as wearing a pin (a popular choice is "I'm Straight but Not Narrow") or writing a letter to the newspaper. For Barry Goldwater, it meant praising his grandson at a statewide rally.

In 1994, the Arizona gay community turned out in force for a Coming Out Day celebration of special significance. Arizona was one of nine states that had recently repelled radical right efforts to qualify an anti-gay initiative for the November ballot. The Arizona opposition had been led by an organization called Arizonans for Fairness, and Barry Goldwater had been its honorary chair. Goldwater was not able to attend the rally, but he sent a letter to be read by Ty, whose voice blended pride and affection as he read his famous grandfather's words:

> To all of you gathered today to support justice, fairness, and equality for gay, lesbian, and bisexual Americans, I greet you and wish I could be there with you. It is appropriate for this rally to be held on the steps of the Supreme Court Building, to help focus attention on the precious American principle of justice. All Americans should be treated equally under the Constitution. The rights and liberties that our founding fathers wrote into the Declaration of Independence and the Constitution were meant for all people. Over time, the Congress and the Supreme Court have been called upon to insure that these basic rights are applied to all Americans. It is time that our nation realized that a significant portion of our society is today excluded and that laws need to be written and enforced to ensure that lesbians and gays are not discriminated against in employment, public accommodations, and housing.

Goldwater hailed the victory of Arizonans for Fairness, expressing particular pleasure in the fact that that its campaign had been supported by most of the state's elected officials. Then he closed on a personal note: "I am especially proud that my grandson, Ty, is reading this letter to you. My love for him, as for all my grandchildren, is strong, and we stand together as a diverse family in our opposition to injustice and inequality."

12

◆

A Survival Guide

Your child has just come out to you. What now?
If you're at all typical, you're not Jeanne Manford or Tom Potter, to whom the disclosure was no more shocking than being informed of their child's favorite singer. You're not Mary Griffith, for whom the revelation evoked visions of hellfire and damnation. You're not Mel Wheatley, who just "knew" that if his son was gay, the stereotypes must be wrong. Nor are you the mother in Houston who says, "When my son told me he was gay, I said, 'How can that be? You're a terrible dresser and you always have holes in your socks.' Every gay man I'd ever known was a snappy dresser."

Still, if you do not share her nonchalance and irony, you probably will share the Houston mother's disbelief. The most common parental reaction to the news is denial. You will probably run through a series of anxious disclaimers: "How can you be sure?" "You haven't dated enough boys (girls)." "This is just a phase you're going through." But by the time children have mustered the courage to come out to parents, they have probably resolved any doubt in their own minds. They are, after all, risking hurt or outright rejection, and are hardly likely to do so on a whim.

While you will need to take care of both yourself and your child, taking care of your son or daughter is the simpler part. No matter how heavy the emotional hit you have absorbed, presumably you still love your child. Children need to hear that. They need to know they are not being ejected from either home or heart—that is probably what they feared most about coming out to you. They don't expect praise and celebration. They know how difficult it was for *them* to accept the fact they're gay, and they are probably prepared to give you time and help to do the same. But they need to know they're still part of the family.

Taking care of yourself can be more complicated. This is especially true if the news comes as a complete surprise, if you've never even considered the possibility of having a gay child. You might feel terrible grief, as if your child had just died. Parents often liken the experience to losing a loved one, frequently passing through similar stages of grief. This seems to happen because in a sense there *has* been a death—of the image of the child that you cherished in your mind.

And grief is just one of the unsettling feelings you might experience. Some of the others are guilt ("What did I do wrong?"), shame ("What will my friends think?"), and anger ("How could you do this to me?"). Whatever form the pain takes, you won't help yourself by suppressing or denying it. It's real, it's normal, and for now you're entitled to it. But you shouldn't have to bear the burden alone. Tell your child that you'd like to discuss the situation with someone you trust: one or more close friends, perhaps, or a minister or rabbi. Tell them what you are feeling, but don't look for magic cures or profound wisdom. Their value right now is simply as sympathetic listeners, outlets for your woe.

Above all, it's important to talk. Some parents carry the burden in silence for years; most of them will tell you it's a brutal form of self-punishment.

You might strike gold in the form of a confidante who has a relative or close friend who is gay, and who can provide you with some truly meaningful insights. But don't count on it. Misinformation on this subject is still rife in our society.

Often, parents fear that telling their good friends might damage their relationships. Judging by the scores of parents I've talked to, that's unlikely. If anything, your friends may be overly sympathetic, tacitly buying into the notion that you and your family have suffered some sort of tragedy. And while an occasional acquaintance might tend to think less of you—well, most parents eventually conclude that such a person wasn't worth calling "friend" anyway.

Desperately seeking someone to "blame"—yourself, your spouse, your child's friends, the schools, the media—is another typical, but wholly unwarranted, response to a child's coming out. While research is beginning to provide some clues, no one yet knows what "causes" homosexuality. But one thing which is certain is that poor parenting is *not* the cause. Nor do children choose to be gay. As writer Richard Mohr points out, picking the gender of a sex partner is quite different from picking a flavor of ice cream. "If people were persecuted, threatened with jail terms, shattered careers, and loss of family and housing and the like for eating, say, Rocky Road ice cream, no one would ever eat it."

Ultimately, you are apt to decide that any notion of blame is inappropriate in this situation—that sexual orientation is no more fit an object of stigma than is hair color or taste in music. In all likelihood, your child has simply recognized a significant facet of his or her personality, the denial of which would jeopardize the attainment of personal well-being. The experience of coming out to oneself is a matter of *discovery*, of peeling away layers of denial and shame. Coming out to you is an act of courage on your child's part. It is also a demonstration of trust in you. Someday, if not now, you'll be grateful for that.

If you can't shake the sense that disaster has struck, be assured that time can do more than merely ease the pain. It can erase it, and actually replace it with joy. To that end, seek out the nearest P-FLAG hotline or support group. If there's none listed in your telephone directory, call the national office (202-638-4200). At

P-FLAG, you'll find caring and understanding—the type of support available only from those who know what you're going through because they have been there themselves. And you'll find the comfort and warmth of solid new friendships.

In a short time, moreover, you will become something of an expert in an area in which most Americans know very little. You may not be out of the closet yet, but you will know that a lot of things other people say about homosexuality are just rumor, innuendo, or misinformation. "Suddenly you're smart in an area where most of the people in the country are just plain dumb," says psychotherapist Cathy Tuerk. "So it helps your self-esteem."

At P-FLAG meetings, you'll also meet lesbians and gay men, and nothing dispels the myths about homosexuality more quickly than meeting people who are ordinary and likable and gay. Through them, you'll gain significant insight into what it's like to grow up gay—and to have to deal with parents who, like you, are unprepared to handle that. Chances are, the experience will increase your respect for your own child.

There are a number of helpful books with up-to-date objective information about homosexuality. Many libraries are expanding their collections on the subject, and P-FLAG can provide you with appropriate titles. But your most meaningful education will probably come from the people you will meet through P-FLAG: other parents, and lesbians and gay men who confound all the stereotypes.

One father at a support group described the process this way: "I see all of us climbing a mountain. The higher we climb, the more we can see. But we're all at different levels. I think I'm somewhere in the middle of the mountain. I started from ignorance, and I still have a long way to go. But I can see much more now than from the bottom of the hill."

At some point in the process, you may become aware that you and your child have reversed roles. You will probably be traveling much the same tortuous path your child has already taken—

and now, your child can teach you. He or she can help you learn what it means—and what it does *not* mean—to be gay, and can help you see the absurdity of many of your lifelong beliefs about homosexuality. Your child can help you understand how rewarding it is for you to look beyond social norms and simply *be* yourself. (As the song "I've Gotta Be Me" puts it, "How can I ever be right for somebody else if I'm not right for me?")

And yes, we even learn more about sexuality itself. For many parents, the most disturbing aspect of a child's homosexuality is imagining their sexual behavior. "I can't bear to think about what they do in the bedroom" is a common support-group lament.

If that's a concern to you, consider some statistics. The boudoir behavior of our gay and lesbian kids, it turns out, is not necessarily all that different from that of their heterosexual siblings. Studies reported by the Kinsey Institute in 1990 indicated that 90 percent of heterosexual couples had engaged in oral sex, and more than a third of American women had had anal sex. A later study reported lower, but still significant, incidences of these practices. Yet, it rarely strikes us to wonder what our heterosexual children might be doing in *their* bedrooms.

"One of the things I find particularly galling," says Mitzi Henderson, P-FLAG's current national president, "is the representation of gay people as being interested in sex as if that's the only thing that's important in their lives. Whenever they're talked about, it's in terms of sexual behavior. And yet when we talk about heterosexual people, we don't talk about adult book stores, prostitution, the sex lives of rock stars, as being typical of heterosexual people."

For those who have not had occasion to consider the prevalence of homosexuality, statistics can afford further surprise. The percentage of Americans who are gay and lesbian is a matter of some controversy. For many years, based on figures contained in the 1948 Kinsey report, the proportion was commonly assumed to be about 10 percent. More recent polls have placed the percentage lower, including at least one that pegged it at a mere 1 percent. Of course, polls have built-in biases: in a society where it is dangerous to be gay, it is not easy to admit homosexuality even to oneself, much less to an inquiring stranger. Most serious researchers—such as those at the Johns Hopkins School of Medicine, where some of the most intensive studies of homosexuality have taken place—estimate the incidence to be at least 6 percent.

Accepting this latter figure as the best available guess, the number of gay people in the country is at least 15 million. Necessarily, those 15 million began life with 30 million parents; and based on national census figures, they have approximately 15 million siblings. Their cousins, aunts, uncles, grandparents, and non-gay friends add up to further millions.

Thus, how we as families and as a society deal with homosexuality is not a narrow concern. It's a fair guess that something like half of all Americans have a reasonably direct stake in the issue. And while tens of thousands of them have taken advantage of P-FLAG support and education resources, tens of *millions* have not.

Of these millions, some are unaware that their child, relative, or friend is gay. Others know or suspect, but prefer to deal with the matter in silence. And many simply have no need for special support, because they are not uncomfortable that someone close to them is gay.

Of those who do find their way to P-FLAG, only a relatively small percentage become activists. Not surprisingly, the typical P-FLAG member is not a Jeanne Manford, Mary Griffith, Bonnie or Buzz Frum, or Elise or Jim Self. To be sure, thousands march in annual gay pride parades around the country as a gesture of parental support; and increasing numbers are speaking out against anti-gay discrimination in radio and television interviews, in their churches, and before city councils, school boards, state legislatures, and community agencies.

But most attend a few P-FLAG meetings and then go on with their lives, their initial concerns lessened or eliminated. They are merely part of a silent army of decent, fair-minded, family-centered citizens. Most people, perhaps an overwhelming majority, are not cut out for activism. But parents of gay children, it seems to me, can't help but harbor at least a degree of righteous anger at those who would diminish their children. My hope is that the anger will someday surface, that the now-silent masses will stand up and make themselves heard.

It's understandable—perhaps inevitable—that parents suffer shock and grief when they first learn of a child's homosexuality. Fathers in particular often find it difficult to express support for a group of citizens commonly derided as "pansies." But their gay kids are in constant jeopardy from a hostile society. Hence, many of these fathers are eventually moved by the parental imperative to stand up for their own.

Jim Pines of Chevy Chase, Maryland, is a thoughtful man who is offended by macho posturing. He says he went through the usual denial, grieving, and other stages so familiar to parents of gay kids. But then came another response, which Jim believes is healthier. It was a combativeness, the fierceness of which astonished him. "In the same way I had always pictured a lion, for example, defending its cubs against the hunter, I found myself enraged that some people might attack my son, verbally or even physically, for something as private and unobjectionable as his sexual orientation.

"I continue to mask my rage, being too 'civilized' to act on it. But I consider my fierce reaction far more appropriate to my masculinity than lamenting my son's homosexuality."

The richest payoffs from adjusting to a child's gayness, however, come in more homespun form.

Pat Romero's face softens when she describes her family's affection for Mike Bieri, her son Mick's mate of twelve years. (For Pat's story, see Chapter 7.) She calls the men's relationship a marriage, and Mike her son-in-law. In actuality, Pat's bond with Mike often seems more that of mother than mother-in-law. His own mother died when he was four, and he has few memories of her. So although Pat is close to the husbands of her two older daughters, there is an added dimension to her relationship with Mike. "I get more hugs from him than I do from Mick," she says.

The closeness of their relationship was never more apparent than when Mick became infatuated with another young man and for a brief time considered breaking up with Mike. Mick asked Pat to talk with Mike about the situation, and they met over coffee. Mike's "dear blue eyes welled up with tears," Pat recalls, as he described how much it meant to him "to come home and there's Mick." But he said what hurt even more was that he wasn't only losing Mick, "I'm losing my family." When Pat passed this on to Mike's three sisters and their husbands, each told Mike that no matter what happened, he would remain part of the family. Indeed, Pat urged Mike to resist Mick's separation plans, which upset Mick. But she told Mick, "You just said talk to him. You did-n't tell me what kind of advice I was supposed to give him."

"Our other daughter, when she comes over with her boyfriend, we expect them to hold hands, snuggle up. If Gina had a lover here, this is her house, she should be accorded the same rights."

Brian Leonard, step-father of Gina Gutierrez, spoke at the kitchen table where he was sitting with Gina's mother, Gloria. Gina, then a senior at Los Gatos High School, was perched on a coun-tertop, legs dangling. Gina had long before told her family she was gay, and a year earlier had made the disclosure to the entire school when she performed a monologue about coming out in the high school auditorium. Now, however, Gloria was feeling reservations about Gina dating other girls while still in high school, and Brian sought to reassure his wife. Placing his hand on hers, he observed gently, "Honey, this is the time kids *are* dating."

This intimate scene is part of a powerful documentary called *Gay Youth* produced by Pam Walton, which has won eight awards and has been shown at film festivals around the world. It features eight gay adolescents, but tiny Gina—high-spirited and elfin, yet thoughtful, articulate, and resolute—is its unquestioned star. And Brian and Gloria fill, as it were, key supporting roles. It is clear that her parents' willingness to accept and appreciate her for who she is are crucial to Gina's confidence, courage, and winning personality.

Some months after the kitchen discussion, Gloria and Gina went shopping for a gown for Gina's senior prom, held in San Francisco. On prom night, Walton filmed Gina and three of her friends in a hotel room they were sharing to dress for the evening.

Gina's date was Cristina Salat. The other two seniors were Gina's close friend Julie Maxson and her date Neil Laslett. In the film, Gina and Cristina are shown comparing their outfits and laughing about how "femme" they will look. Then, while Gina applies polish to Julie's nails, Julie speaks to the camera about her schoolmate. She doesn't think of Gina as a lesbian, she says, but simply as "Gina my friend." And she praises Gina's openness about her orientation. "I don't know if I could do something like that." The prom-night vignette ends with a shot of Gina and Cristina's formal photograph: two elegantly gowned young women, beaming before a festive backdrop of brightly colored balloons.

The film's climax focuses on Gina's graduation. At the awards ceremony, Brian and Gloria watch proudly as Gina receives a $500 scholarship award for her work with gay and lesbian issues. (The award, co-sponsored by P-FLAG and a Bay Area gay teachers group, was named in memory of Mary Griffith's son Bobby.) Then, at commencement, as she strode across the platform to receive her diploma, the announcement of her name triggered a noisy ovation from her fellow students.

At the end, the camera catches a teary Gina in long embraces with her mother and step-father. Then they all burst into laughter as Gina reveals that she had been given a blank diploma: "I forgot to turn in a textbook."

*   *   *

A member of my P-FLAG chapter, a white-haired former elementary school teacher, likes to talk about her living arrangement. Like many other older single women, she lives in a cozy mother-in-law apartment in her son's Victorian house.

That her son's partner is another man does not make these circumstances any less ordinary. She and the couple go pretty much their separate ways, following her golden rule of intergenerational living: "I don't smother them, and they don't smother me." But the men are there to help her with heavy tasks, she takes pleasure in doing occasional household errands for them while they're at work, and dinner together in her apartment is a ritual on holidays.

Friends regularly urge her to move to a nearby retirement development with its broad range of senior activities. But she likes being with her family. She loves "my two sons," who have lived together for twenty years and spend much of their spare time working on the stately old Victorian house they have owned since 1977. She is fond of the tree-lined block of trim turn-of-the-century houses on which they live, with its friendly neighbors and many youngsters. (A lover of children, but with no grandchildren of her own, she counts herself "the third grandmother" of numerous tots.) And she's available when the men are looking for company at a movie or some special gathering.

"It's a comfortable arrangement," she says. "I can't imagine myself living anywhere else."

In November 1994, a *New York Times* article by critic John O'Connor described the growing presence of gay characters and gay issues on television. Among other examples, he cited "an extraordinary documentary called *Straight from the Heart*, profiling parents who have developed a new understanding of their gay and lesbian children." Produced by Dee Mosbacher (see Chapter 11) and Frances Reid, the film features a number of P-FLAG families discussed in this book.

One of the film's emotional highlights is a spontaneous out-burst of affection in which Mildred Washington's twin daughters, both lesbian, smother her in hugs and kisses and peals of laughter. The playful display was touched off by Mildred's obviously heartfelt tribute to Sandra and Sharon. "I'm very proud of my daughters," she said. "There is nothing they have ever done that I am not proud of." Pausing to look at them, she added, "I'm proud of their accomplishments. I'm proud of their independence. I'm proud of the way they have always respected me and other adults and people their own age. I'm just proud of my daughters. I think they're the two most wonderful people in the world."

The Washingtons are African American, a fact that complicated family acceptance of the girls' lesbianism. Some relatives saw homosexuality as "a white disease" and said the twins must have picked it up from white people. Others insisted that American blacks cannot be gay, since they're all descended from slaves chosen for strength, virility, and childbearing capacity.

The twins' father, moreover, was a Hall of Fame miler at Ohio State who spent thirty years with the Department of Defense—a background that left him quite unprepared to accept gay children. But Donald Washington also loved young people—he spent most of his spare time in volunteer youth work—and had become enthusiastically supportive of his daughters for some years before his death in 1990.

To Mildred, a retired guidance counselor, acceptance was ultimately just a matter of common sense. Learning of the girls' orientation disturbed her. But was it a problem because they were gay, she asked herself, or because she was ashamed to tell her friends? "And all the answers came back to the problem lies with me, not them."

The twins, now thirty-four, have indeed given Mildred much to be proud of. Sandra is a planner with the National Park Service in Lincoln, Nebraska. Sharon is a professor at Kent State. Together, they form a professional singing team that has been featured at

African-American and gay community events since 1983. Each is on the telephone with Mildred at least three times a week.

Being gay does not affect innate longings associated with ritual and tradition. Mildred's eyes twinkle as she recalls, "As a kid, Sandra always had a hope chest." And several months after the documentary was filmed, Sandra fulfilled her longstanding dream—she and her mate of five years, Deb Cirksena, were formally united in a church ceremony. A Congregational minister did the honors, and family members on both sides attended. Sharon was Sandra's best woman, and Mildred sang a duet with Deb's mother, a medley of "I Believe" and "Ave Maria."

Accounts of gay wedding ceremonies are becoming staple fare in gay community newspapers. The rites unfortunately have no legal standing, but that hardly lessens the accompanying celebrations. And increasingly, parents and other family members are among the celebrants, echoing Mildred Washington's pronouncement about her daughter's rites: "It was a wonderful, wonderful ceremony."

Pat and Dan Stone's 1994 Christmas card was a family portrait taken on the porch of their ranch home in Dallas. Pat, Dan, and son Brad stand grinning behind the porch swing. Seated on the swing are daughter TJ and her partner Katherine Allen. On the young women's laps are the Stones' two grandsons: Matt, who is seven, and Zack, born just eight months before.

The accompanying four-page letter from Dan explained that Matt is Katherine's son by an earlier marriage and that Zack is the Stones' first biological grandchild. TJ and Katherine have been together for six years; and Zack's biological father, Keith Hyatte, is the thirteen-year partner of Katherine's brother, John Allen. Keith has no legal or financial responsibility for Zack, but he and John consider themselves part of the family. "Of course," Dan wrote, "when TJ told us that she intended to get pregnant, she had to slow down and explain a lot of this to me."

Dan said his message was written for those friends who might not already be aware of the Stones' extended family. He explained, "By sending this letter with each card, everyone knows that everyone else has been posted. This may make it a little easier for you to open a discussion about the subject with others. There's no need to be secretive about this; we're certainly not."

When she was younger, TJ had told her parents that she wasn't going to "marry some guy and move far away." She kept part of the promise—she moved far away (to Virginia), but with a woman.

"And quite a woman she is," Dan wrote in his letter. "Katherine is a warm, caring person, a university professor and the loving life-partner of TJ. When the law allows it, they'll be married. We love Katherine and Matt and accept them as full members of our family. We benefit from their love."

Dan's message pointed out that gay people are often denied their full rights as citizens. However hard it is to comprehend, he wrote, gays are losing their jobs and even being killed, simply because they are gay:

> I hope you get the message. It's one that shouldn't be put in the closet. It needs talking about. I care about what you think or I would never have sent you this letter. I love my daughter, and I admire her and have been enriched by her life experiences. I accept her without any reservation, and I want you to accept her and her family with the warmth that you have always extended to me. That's my Christmas wish.

These families have overcome the impediments raised by social prejudice—and the best gauge of their victory is the ordinariness with which they view their gay family members. We like to feel that's the way it is in our family, too.

My daughter Bobbi has been in a committed relationship since 1989 with Donna Hylton, a systems analyst living in suburban

Washington, D.C. For Myrna and me, and for Bobbi's mother and grandmother, embracing a same-sex couple in the family circle was hardly an immediate response. But our adjustment to what now seems commonplace was aided by the relaxed attitudes of our other children. Unlike most older people, many of today's young adults have known gay people in school, work, and social settings; and to them, the gender of a loved one's mate can be a matter of little moment. Fortunately, for us, that's how it was with Bobbi's siblings.

Thanks to them and their mates, Bobbi and Donna are just another of the couples in our family—no big deal. Bobbi's closest friend has always been her older sister, Sharon. Both daughters have always related to Myrna's two sons, Douglas and Dietrich Nebert, as brothers rather than step-brothers. And Bobbi's coming out produced nary a ripple in any of the relationships.

Bobbi is now completing her last year at Stanford Law School before returning to live with Donna and work in Washington. While at Stanford, she spends virtually every weekend with Sharon and her mate, John Sheehan, who live in nearby Oakland.

Frequently, Donna flies in to visit Bobbi; then all four of the young people get together. And one Thanksgiving, they were all joined by Dietrich, then living in Oregon, who drove six hundred miles to stay with Bobbi and share the holiday with his family. On Thanksgiving Day, they all pitched in to prepare dinner at Sharon and John's. Then they all got sick together, apparently because the oven malfunctioned and the turkey was undercooked. But the "turkey trot," as they called it, has become part of family lore—the kind of shared adversity that somehow over time becomes amusing.

If Bobbi and Donna are just another pair in the extended clan, they have nevertheless added an important dimension to our family calculus.

For one thing, Bobbi and Donna are the only couple for whom the rest of the family regularly feels moved to express public support. One way we do this is by marching in gay pride parades. The throng of Bobbi's relatives usually includes her grandmother and even, in one instance, Doug's nine-month-old son.

The mere presence of Bobbi and Donna within the family circle has other effects. For example, Doug and his wife Dee Ann say that Bobbi and Donna serve a kind of special education function for their three children. For however hate-free a home might be, youngsters cannot wholly avoid society's anti-gay cast. So when their twelve-year-old daughter expressed disapproval about a gay couple in a movie, Dee Ann and Doug had a ready response. They reminded her that her own family includes such a pair, Bobbi and Donna, whom she likes and admires.

Of course, when I proclaim the ordinariness of having a gay couple in the family, I'm engaging in a certain amount of self-contradiction. If it really were ordinary, I wouldn't be writing about it. Marching in support of the rights of Bobbi and Donna would have no more meaning than marching for those of Sharon and John. Dan Stone would feel no need to send a four-page explanation with his Christmas card. Mildred Washington's motherly declaration of pride in her two daughters would merit a mere shrug rather than inclusion in a documentary.

Still, our experiences, and those of countless others, prove that gay children *can* fit seamlessly into the family circle. However strong your initial shock, you'll probably soon realize that your son or daughter is the same person he or she was before coming out to you—as worthy of your love now as before. You may need some help to get to the point of easy acceptance—from P-FLAG or some other sympathetic source—but you can get there. And when you arrive, you and your family will be whole once more.

13

♦

A Call to Arms

Vic Basile is a leading gay activist. His father, Jimmy Basile,
is a Catholic-Italian, second-generation party precinct
worker in an industrialized New England neighborhood.
"That fits a stereotype of someone you'd expect to be a bigot," Vic
says. And when Vic came out to his parents in 1981, Jimmy
seemed to go into shock. Although his mother was instantly supportive, "for Dad it was pure trauma."

The love of politics runs in the family. During much of the
1980s, Vic was executive director of a gay lobby group, the
Human Rights Campaign Fund; under his leadership, it became
one of the nation's largest independent political action committees.
An important turning point in his father's attitude toward gay
people was a black-tie HRCF dinner in Washington, D.C. to which
Vic invited his parents. Vic knew that Jimmy still harbored some
stubborn stereotypes; and he hoped that the sight of hundreds of
successful, well-dressed lesbians and gay men from all professions
and careers might help change those images.

Vic was nervous about one matter. He warned his parents they
would be seeing something new for them: the sight of men greeting each other by kissing. "Mother said, 'Okay, fine,'" Vic remembers. "But Dad said nothing. I could see he was edgy about it. That
made me even jumpier."

At the dinner, father and son were both tense for the first few minutes as Vic began introducing Jimmy to his acquaintances. Then, after about the fourth person, Jimmy kissed every man Vic introduced him to!

Jimmy had a grand time that night. He even met one of his longtime political heroes, openly gay Massachusetts congressman Barney Frank. And some months later came a vivid demonstration of how Jimmy's feelings about Vic's gayness had changed. Jimmy was interviewed for a newspaper feature story about his longtime political activity; and he made a special point of telling the reporter to write how proud he was of his gay son.

The sentiment is roundly returned. Vic's voice catches as he tells that story about the change in attitude of a "very Catholic" elderly man with a macho ethnic heritage. "It was very touching for me to see this happen," Vic says. "It's a very remarkable thing he did."

Icy stereotypes have a way of thawing when exposed to real-life openly gay and lesbian people. The same point was made by Mel Wheatley to his fellow bishops, and by Wayne Schow to his fellow Mormons: Homosexuality isn't about morals or theology, it's about people. Very frequently, they are people who are vital, creative, caring, and interesting—people you feel fortunate, sometimes even honored, to know. When you meet them, the stereotypes suddenly no longer make sense. And if you get to know them well, it can even change your life.

Not long after my introduction to P-FLAG, my earlier prejudice toward gay people was turned on its head. I came to believe that many of them were actually better people for being openly gay—for daring to be themselves. It's like the point of an old Hasidic story about a Rabbi Zusya, who went to heaven expecting to be asked, "Why weren't you more like Moses?" Instead, he was asked, "Why weren't you more like Rabbi Zusya?"

In P-FLAG, we have the privilege of sharing in the triumphs and setbacks of young people as they confront the challenge of being themselves. We admire their courage in facing up to it.

And we are warmed by the aura of joy that accompanies their success.

Moreover, as the stories in this book illustrate, parents often experience a similar sense of liberation. For we face our own challenges and fears, the overcoming of which can lead to new levels of sensitivity and self-awareness. The words *joy* and *liberation* are spoken often at P-FLAG meetings by parents as well as gays.

I heartily second Mel Wheatley's observation that his life has been incredibly enriched by knowing gay and lesbian people. I know that society's lingering cruelty will cause hardships for my daughter. But a life without struggle is hardly worth the name. And her struggle will be shared with a community that is long on wisdom, warmth, and compassion.

Perhaps I shouldn't ask for more. But I do. Expanding awareness has brought impatience:

- Impatience with the hypocrisy of some churches and church leaders who preach love but practice oppression.
- Impatience with school officials who deny teenagers the courses and counseling that could save them from despair, addiction, and death.
- Impatience with a court system that says it is constitutional to jail people for the physical expression of their love.
- Impatience with a military system that wastes taxpayer money while scarring the lives of able, brave Americans.
- Impatience with those who find riches and power in homophobic pandering to the childlike religiosity of their emotionally insecure idolaters.
- Impatience with politicians at every level who allow their votes to be swayed by demagogues of bigotry.
- And, I confess, impatience with parents who are slow to speak out on behalf of their gay and lesbian children.

Shortly after Bobbi told me she was a lesbian, I had a dream. It was a dream of an uprising of tens of millions of parents insisting on an end to society's cruelty toward their gay kids. Instinctual parental love, I thought, would inevitably lead these legions to reject the nonsense that clutters the national mindset. It would, I reasoned, quickly convert them to crusaders for justice and the celebration of cultural diversity. The result, I envisioned, would be a sea change in social attitudes toward homosexuality and gay people.

Eight years later, I sometimes have difficulty keeping the dream in focus.

To be sure, a cadre of uncloseted and sometimes outspoken parents does exist, and its numbers, however slowly, are growing. As I write, P-FLAG has more than three hundred groups and contacts throughout the country. We *shall* overcome. But the moment of triumph is considerably farther down the road, and more difficult of achievement, than my first flush of enthusiasm led me to believe.

Too often, it turns out, the force of parental love is simply no match for that of societal bigotry. Many parents of gay kids are themselves so oppressed—by pseudo-religious moralism, by their own inner sexual terrors, by peer pressure—that they shrink from personal enlightenment as from some dread demon. In gratuitous panic and rage, they disown their gay children. Or by a type of spiritual dismissal that is just as hurtful, they simply refuse to acknowledge an important part of their children's essential being.

Others, while more enlightened, profess not to see the importance of taking a public stand. They are perhaps personally accepting of their children's gayness, and acknowledge the falsity of conventional stereotypes. Nevertheless, they are unwilling to pay the price—vastly inflated in their minds—of departing their relatively comfortable closets. For them, the craving for peer approval may command a higher priority. The imagined responses of others can carry the day.

I don't rule out the possibility, though, that the single most important factor may simply be the old enemy—apathy—fed by a lack of awareness of the impact that every parent can make.

The oppression of our children is kept alive in large part by the big lie. In their book *After the Ball,* Marshall Kirk and Hunter Madsen define this as the widespread assumption that gays are "rare freaks." This is the notion that homosexuality, while a product of sin and/or sickness, is nevertheless sufficiently rare that it can be ignored by "proper" folk.

If the big lie is to be countered, parents of gay children must play a key role. The prejudice of centuries won't be eliminated overnight, but it cannot long survive a concerted challenge by those of us with gay loved ones.

Do you have a gay child, relative, or friend? Enlist in the fight to unmask the big lie.

You have nothing to lose but a musty, uncomfortable closet.

Index

◆